RESCUE *from* DOMESTIC PERFECTION

RESCUE
from
DOMESTIC PERFECTION

THE *Not-So* SECRETS *of* BALANCING LIFE *and* STYLE

DAN HO

BULFINCH PRESS
NEW YORK • BOSTON

Bulfinch Press

Hachette Book Group USA

1271 Avenue of the Americas, New York, NY 10020

Visit our Web site at www.bulfinchpress.com

First Edition: October 2006

Library of Congress Catalogin-in-Publication Data

Ho, Dan.
  Rescue from domestic perfection: the not-so secrets of balancing life and style / Dan Ho.—1st ed.
      p. cm.
  Includes index.
  ISBN-10: 0-8212-5803-6 (trade pbk.)
  ISBN-13: 978-0-8212-5803-3 (trade pbk.)
  1. Interior decoration. 2. Interior decoration—Psychological aspects. I. Title.

NK2115.H487 2006
747—dc22   2005031104

Designed by Kay Schuckhart/Blond on Pond

Printed in China

For Dad. For Mom.

CONTENTS

Perfection is a cheap

caricature of style.

—Dan Ho

INTRODUCTION

Where perfection goes, nonsense is sure to follow.

And style ain't nowhere to be seen, neither.

I'm hardly a statistician, nor does this book purport to present the results of some major study on useless junk as it exists in America's homes. Still, I'm willing to bet that the average person reading this book (or one who has ventured into the aisle in the bookstore where it is located) has some collection of scented candles, vases, or glue-gun sticks that are doing little else but gathering dust. Stuff that'll probably never come out of its dark corners except for a once-in-a-blue-moon appearance for a never-to-be-had-again reason — in other words, that perfect moment.

One of the curiosities of our contemporary lifestyle is the glaringly huge disconnect that exists between what we know and how we live. Take baking, for example. We know that buying flour in bulk saves money, time, and energy — so we do it. Yet we have little, if any, hesitation about wantonly disregarding the gain from this knowledge by spending more money, time, and energy putting that flour into some container that conveniently matches the sugar jar, pasta jar, and bean jar. Then, to accomodate the display potential of said containers, we appropriate even more money, time, and energy to procure merchandising-appropriate cabinets, drawers, and counter-tops. And so it goes: the appliances require a certain look and quality; all of a sudden your perfectly fine plastic measuring cups seem wrong, and in march the new stainless-steel ones. One day you encounter grilled bread, and your life and its accoutrements change again. You spend days, weeks, maybe months, finding the right bread-grilling tools. Someone (bless them) gifts you with the perfect bread knife — the kind the bakers at Poilane in Paris use. But what becomes of the old bread knife? Furthermore, the new one doesn't fit in the knife block. Witness how a seemingly small perfection turns into a mountain of nonsense.

Mercifully, you're too busy giving away holiday gifts of homemade Linzer tortes to worry about it (although you make a mental note: "Gotta find a new knife block"). The twistedly organic thought comes to mind: there's no such thing as patisserie cards and gift wrap. So you outfit a craft kit and load up on the card stock and ribbons in order to properly present the fruits of your labor and give evidence that you know how to buy flour cheaply.

Of course, at this point a craft room is inevitable (as though it were remotely logical that baking would beget a space entirely devoted to creating disposable mementos). You can't help but envision a wall of perfectly sized cubbyholes for your glorious paperie but fail to ponder the effects of the Atkins and South Beach diets on your mini-industry. Nobody wants your pastry anymore — the flour is killing them. What do you do? Switch to beef jerky, starting off with bulk beef buys and a walk-in meat locker? Oy. Vey.

The cycle of perfection is unending. Worse, it is downright insidious. How'd you get from baking to craft room? Did it begin because a financial guru said that buying in bulk saves money? Was it because you liked the way sugar looked in jars at Williams-Sonoma? Be very aware: when people lose their singularly distinct personal resonances with objects in their lives, the latter become irrelevant. This is sad but true.

For the record, I personally have nothing against things that don't end. Yet the constant pursuit of lifestyle perfection has no payoff that accompanies it. Love gets you compassion, and a healthy heart gives you longevity. The perfect set of dining-room chairs offers, at best, a fleeting satisfaction — let's face it, they're only going to be perfect as long as nothing changes. And so here lies the essential problem with the notion of perfection: it is unmoving, inanimate, incapable of evolution.

Life, alas, is entirely about change: fabrics and paint pigments fade, roofs leak, carpets and floors get stained. In fact, dining tables as a concept have gone in and out of fashion at least twice in my adult life. When you pursue the trappings of a home where you can cook, entertain, and garden perfectly, you get zilch. You don't even get style — there, I said it.

Perfection is a cheap caricature of style, which is why committing to it is nonsense. You can fill your home with things every decorating diva has deemed must-have; you can cook all your food in the manner of celebrity chefs; you can edge your perennial borders in a manner that emulates that of the chief groundskeeper at Kew Gardens. But these will all be pointless style exercises unless and until you understand what style really means. It is my hope that you will gain that understanding in this book.

Rest assured, this ain't no makeover. The first place to start is inside — rather than worrying about how things look, coordinate, taste, and smell, simply start thinking about who you are inside. If you can do this much, I promise you will be well on your way to true style.

PART I

PHILOSOPHY

gai

My philosophy is easily expressed by these few words: **your spirit is your style. I call this philosophy *gai*, which is a Chamorro verb that approximates "is there now."**

Chamorro is a term that describes all things from Guam, which is where I was born. As a native of Guam, I am Chamorro. The little-known language of the natives, which I speak, is Chamorro. Chamorro is to Guam what Welsh is to Wales, what Yankee is to New England. I'm Guamanian as much as a chap from the Netherlands is Netherlandian. No such thing, right? He's Dutch. I'm Chamorro.

As you probably already know, the English language lacks many cut-and-dried equivalents for certain foreign words, for example, *taboo*. Up until this Polynesian term fell upon the ears of westerners, English speakers lacked a word to describe inhibition or aversion to specific behaviors or objects. *Gai* is similar to *taboo* in this way — it does not have an easily identified English counterpart. In its most elementary form, *gai* can mean the same as *have,* except that it is used exclusively to indicate qualitative traits such as respect or honor. More accurately, it assists in articulating the supernatural or spiritual nature of an individual, time, or place. In this sense it departs from the relatively democratic persuasions of the verb *to have;* rather, it actualizes a singular expression of the individual's condition in the universe. You might call it a sacred verb.

The closest translation of *gai* — "is there now" — is what prompted my adaptation of it to describe my philosophy. The implication in "The lights are on, but no one's home" is not dissimilar to the metaphor of *gai*. As a lifestyle philosophy, *gai* challenges us to "check in" with ourselves before we start to decorate, cook, garden, dress, or entertain.

Don't we all know people who have the perfect jobs, to which they go every morning dressed in a perfect wardrobe while tossing their perfectly coiffed hair? We may know others who live in perfect houses with chef's kitchens, weedless green lawns, and golden retrievers that actually heel. Lately, through the grotesque and boundaryless wonders of television, we've encountered women with

couple in the terminal And if I'm being honest, I wouldn't have noticed them except that first-class passengers were called to board first — and you just have to look at the lucky ones, the other half, as it were. At least I do.

Invariably, some sass-and-a-half lady flying economy with too-big hair and a pocketbook that never made anyone's best-dressed list strikes me as interesting. Something about

Sure, they're billboards for the ambush wardrobe-makeover show. They're also entirely forgettable.

brand-new lips, new chests, liposuctioned stomachs, and surgically perfected noses. These are people who are easily categorized by the so-called quality of their trappings, but that's the extent of our recognition of them — they're just a type. Would we, in fact, recognize them outside their picture-perfect worlds? Would they be the same people to us if they were janitors, or cooked in their circa-1969 avocado/lime kitchens, or kept their flat chests and quirky noses?

This happens to me all the time: I'll people-watch at an airport and casually notice a couple traveling "in style." She'll be in a pastel-colored cashmere twinset and expensive shoes, toting a pricey bag that she carries like a trophy. He'll be in two-hundred-dollar khakis and a golf shirt, busily manipulating his BlackBerry. Clearly, they've checked off the season's list of must-haves; yet to me, in that moment, they are the most visually boring

her is irresistible; I can't quite put my finger on it. I am forced to look past all the things that makeover divas would deem fashion no-nos — her straight-legged jeans, her shoulder pads, her blue eyeliner — and made to recognize her as an individual. Why should I care, never mind be charmed by her? It is because her spirit is her style, not her clothes, hair, or accessories. She's got, as I say, *gai*.

By now I've forgotten about the couple in first class who've done everything "right." My brain is barely interested in retaining a memory of them, because their spirit — who they are — is not apparent on the outside. Sure, they're billboards for the ambush wardrobe-makeover show. They're also entirely forgettable.

OPPOSITE: It's entirely okay to be concerned about what people think of you; it's a part of the system we call human nature. To work the system best, let go of the facade in favor of deeper meaning, which is ultimately what style is.

Gai happens when you are more interesting than your stuff. *Gai* is neither rich nor poor. Indeed, if you weren't in touch with your spirit when you bought your eight-thousand-dollar sofa — specifically, that the pressure to conform guided its purchase — it's as much nonsense as a rat's nest in an abandoned city lot. Mother Teresa, the poorest philanthropist who ever lived, had *gai,* as does Cher, whose personality outshines any expensive, tacky Mackie she dons. Sarah Jessica Parker is a great example of *gai.* We are enchanted by her style not because of what's on the outside; she'll probably be the first to admit she's far from a supermodel in physicality. And she wears, quite frankly, stuff that most women find scary. Yet she could be wearing a paper bag and rubber bands, and she'd still be photographed for some fashion roundup. Her spirit is her style. We see *gai* in Bono and David Bowie, but there are many supercool people in everyday life who have it. Simply look at black women going to church on Sundays or little kids on a playground. But don't turn on the cooking or home channels, where any kind of individuality is virtually absent.

Similarly, there are supremely atypical (i.e., imperfect) interiors and exteriors that are sacred in the annals of style iconography. The fabled dark red walls of Diana Vreeland's

TOP: Me at age two. When I look at this picture I wonder what the heck I was thinking. I must have been a scary toddler. **BOTTOM:** I'm between my older, identical twin brothers, Sam [left] and Joe [right]. We're on my mother's red Naugahyde love seat. A red couch is something that's been a constant in my life.

apartment are a statement most would be too weak to make, as are the transparent walls the world recognizes as Philip Johnson's glass house. There are thousands of ostensibly fabulous châteaus in France, but can we name one, two, or three of them? Untold numbers of priceless paintings exist in the world's museums and in private collections, yet it's the rule breakers who occupy our attentions. Monet, Warhol, Pollock, Kahlo. They all broke from the

fore the wrong place to start. In fact, I am loath to be known just as some kind of nauseating expert on homes/food/gardening/entertaining who didn't stand for something. Gag me with a garlic press! Style comes from life, so we have to begin with mine.

Something big occurred in 1998 that forced me to concede the true meaning of style. I had to accept finally that there were far more important things in life than proper risotto

Gai happens when you are more interesting than your stuff.

standard of perfection at their time. Really, who gives a shake about the blur of perfectly executed shoji screens or the excruciatingly photographed landscapes of the Wyeths? Where are their movies and bestselling books?

Gai is the state at which who you are inside is undeniable style on the outside. As an aesthetic, it's unlike minimalism or "country" or "cottage style." You can achieve true style in a double-wide trailer or in a multimillion-dollar mansion. True style — *gai* — is a way of thinking. One simply has to remember that being stylish is little more than knowing what matters most in life. And how do I know this, you ask? Well, some funny stuff happened on my road to being here now.

MY STORY: THE EARLY YEARS

I can't launch into this book by immediately discussing organization, color, proportion, and texture. All of that stuff by itself tends to be trite and meaningless nonsense and is there-

technique, my precious three-acre garden, and the quality of beeswax that went into my candles. Something equally profound had happened in 1976, which I'll speak of later, but let me admit now that during the twenty-two years that followed, I had been caught up in overachievement. I'd spent many years defining for myself what success in America meant, which, back then, was (and still is) the opinion of others regarding what my house looked like. It wasn't enough to be grateful that I'd beaten the odds by becoming a successful millionaire entrepreneur by age thirty in Chicago's competitive restaurant scene.

I was born and raised in Guam, an island on the farthest edge of the western Pacific Ocean that few people, even today, think about. People always ask me what it was like growing up there. Surely I've answered honestly every time, yet as I write this, I struggle to simplify the complexities of that experience in a manner that isn't reduced to irrelevant melodrama. My revelations will absolutely help you become a better home dweller — I promise. Please remember this commitment as I regale you with the salient bits.

I learned right off the bat that my existence would probably be more difficult than interesting. My parents, Rosa and Daniel, were child prisoners of war during the brutal Japanese occupations of World War II. They raised my three brothers, two sisters, and me in a home that most Americans would consider impoverished. It was built of raw, unpainted concrete, wood, tin sheeting, and Masonite. The plumbing was exposed; every faucet and showerhead in the house was an outdoor spigot. There were two bedrooms — my sisters had the privacy. The walls were covered in crayon, pen, and pencil markings; the checkered tiled floors were filmy from years of washing. Every now and then during termite season, we'd huddle in the middle of the main room, holding up a bowl of water and a flashlight to mitigate the Hitchcockian swarms that made their way indoors. We simply could not keep them out. Or the geckos.

Yet there were many gloriously incongruous privileges. Having survived the horrors of war, my parents valued above all else passion, love, family, education, music, well-made food, and good looks. So instead of things like house paint and shower curtains, we got music lessons. Instead of a proper master bedroom, my parents bought not one but two encyclopedia sets and opted to behave like young lovers on the couch when they thought we were all asleep. Rather than replacing the threadbare sofa, a less ragged sheet went on it while we attended private school and groomed with French hair products. We slept on World War II infantry cots. Mother's container plantings were executed in the hollow bellies of drab green bombshells. Her prized collection of orchids grew in beds of rusted tin sheeting, crumpled chicken wire, and the discarded tire rims from old military trucks. The cutlery, utensils, and cooking pots were furnished from the finest government-issued stainless steel, which she bought at auction at the Naval Supply Depot. I was already a big boy when our first Christmas tree came into the house, but I can't tell you exactly when I could differentiate the rare, naturally talented cook from one who was merely well trained. I always knew — I can still tell a know-it-all from a God-gifted chef in one or two bites. This ability to discern is one of many strange skills my parents passed on to me, even on the desperate mornings before payday when we'd have to scour the house for pennies for school lunch. Mom would joke out loud that she hoped the food was worth it.

Considering the general state of the world's population, my childhood was hardly devoid of hedonistic pleasures; people had and have it much worse. The difficulties were emotional ones, of the ilk regularly endured by outsiders or outcasts, which, oddly enough, we were. For one thing, we were mestizo, my mother a blood native, my father a Visayan Filipino who left his family's war-ravaged fish farms as a teenager to seek out his destiny in America (its closest point of entry being Guam). My mother was a divorcée with babies who boldly left a physically abusive arranged marriage

TOP: Me and Mom. We both decided to take off our glasses because the glare from her plastic tablecloth reflected too much in the lenses.

OPPOSITE: My dad in 1976. He is my ultimate style influence. He wanted to be (and was) buried in his caramel-colored boots. The shirt he's wearing is in my closet today.

set up by her father who was firmly devout in ancient native tradition. She and my father met and "shacked up" when my older sisters were twenty months old and newborn. My mother was an only child, my father alone. This, too, was strange. We did not enjoy the familial goodwill that regular Chamorro families had with their large extended families. Our sins and shortcomings could not be buffered by protective uncles and first cousins; our honor was always something to prove face-to-face. We were alone and different. As kids, we were vulnerable.

The pain, if it existed, resulted from the conspiracies of catty neighbors who lived in painted houses or nuns who took pleasure in mispronouncing the name my parents proudly placed on my birth certificate, Daniel Dumdum, Jr. That's right: D-u-m-d-u-m. It was pronounced "Doom-doom," but corrections were a futile exercise even more humiliating than being called Dumb-dumb in the first place. I'd come home crying, and my parents would boost me, coaching me with "Tell them not — could not — obliterate my instinct to get on, and to get even by getting better.

Even if I wanted to crawl into a hole and die, my parents would have none of it. Their musical sons were regularly dispatched in service to the parish. My older brothers, Sam and Joe, who were identical twins, served all the special masses as an exquisitely handsome matching pair of altar boys. They were catcher and pitcher for the parish pony league and were present at all events that could benefit from the novelty of look-alikes. I played the piano for the Sunday masses and weddings,

> *I will never choose a sofa, a shirt, or a color of paint because someone else said it was "of the moment." Forget that.*

they're dumb! Dumb is spelled with a *b*." It was a good idea for a while, until a bitchy nun who taught math asked me to stand up in front of class one day, posing a question.

"Daniel, when two or more numbers are added, what is the outcome called?"

"It's called the sum, Sister," I replied confidently, respectfully.

"Can you spell it for us, Daniel?" she asked.

"S-u-m," I answered.

"What, no *b*?" she asked flatly.

The class roared with laughter, which she allowed to die down slowly and naturally. After a few minutes she told me that I could sit back down. This went on for several years. While they were assuredly awful, these episodes did though long before that, I was pushed to enter islandwide speech and writing contests on behalf of the very parish that emotionally tortured us. To this day, my baby brother, Reu, lends his musical talents to the village faithful — as do all the members of his band, which includes his own identical twin sons. My sisters, Mary and Jessica, accompanied my mother to rosaries and novenas around the village, assisting in Chamorro prayer and song. Hell, the parish school's library was built by none other than my resolute dad.

It's incredible to think that it took nearly thirty years for the parish to okay my mother's annulment so she could enjoy a girlish wish: to marry my father in the village church. When

that happened, Mom and Dad exchanged vows surrounded by their children, all of adult age except for seventeen-year-old me and fourteen-year-old Reu. I wore a silver lamé tuxedo jacket, which my dad declared plenty appropriate for the daytime. It had been made for my prom a week earlier. The wedding feast was at the House of Chin Fee, a greasy chopstick diner. By 1984, my parents' personal and financial lots had greatly improved. They'd built a sturdy new home four years earlier, complete with a private master bedroom, where they spent their wedding night. We teased them to be careful not to let us catch them on the living-room floor.

If we won respect in the village, the world that was opening up to us was not so quick to lend it up front. We were dumb-dumbs in the mainland U.S.A., too. After a particularly upsetting incident that befell brother Joe, my father finally relented to my mother's pleading that the children take his mother's name, the beautiful, French-sounding Drilon. This was a huge personal concession on my dad's part, I believe. He knew who he was and wanted his children to be as proud of, if committed to, its bracing singularity. He knowingly exploited the name as he rose in rank in his chosen field (civil engineering and construction) in a way he couldn't have done were his name just plain and pretty. Long after his retirement, to many in his peer group, Danny Dumdum still means individuality, strength, integrity, intelligence, compassion, élan.

Legacy is another one of those precious family lessons. Indeed, it is something that is

RESCUE

STYLE IS KNOWING WHAT MATTERS THE MOST

vol #7 JAN FEB 2005

Magazine

WIN CASH & COOL PRIZES

INSIDE LEMON CAPER SAUCE DINNERS WITH GRAM COAT BUTTONS HOUSEPLANTS LACE AND MORE

Love makes things match.

Amour before Décor

I believed in my message so much that I started my own magazine with my own money called *Rescue Magazine: Relief from House, Garden, and Food Perfection*. It was very well received by the public and media. I'm grateful that my Dad lived to see me mentioned in *Time* and *USA Today*.

close to my spirit, and it informs every style statement I make. I will never choose a sofa, a shirt, or a color of paint because someone else said it was "of the moment." Forget that. And when I choose, I will ask myself, "Can this be useful to someone else when I am done with it?" Truly, if I were hit by a bus, I'd like the stranger who caught my dying breath to think, "Great boots! He must have been really cool."

In 1976, when I was nine, one of the largest supertyphoons in history, Typhoon Pamela, hit Guam. My siblings, parents, and I descended into our storm cellar, a seven-by-ten poured-concrete basement, to wait out the storm. For eight hours, the cellar shook as though trains were running on tracks overhead. We could hear the wind scream outside. We prayed; my sisters and we little ones cried. It was pretty awful.

In the morning my parents led us outside. We walked up the concrete stairs to what should have been the kitchen, but it was gone. We were standing on what was left of the floor; we should have been inside but were very much outdoors. The house had completely disappeared! We were speechless.

behind our house. But none of it stopped my parents from being gracious hosts. They'd invite neighbors to bring their laundry to the riverbank, and whenever there was a guitar around, Mom would sing. Now, that's what I call entertaining. Tablescapes, themes, party favors — they are empty gestures in the absence of sharing your heart and soul with others.

I understood, right then and there, that for the rest of my life my notion of home would have nothing to do with the house.

I looked down the Agat Valley and out to the calm ocean and the unspeakably blue sky. I could have easily daydreamed or run around with my siblings to rummage through the scant debris. But something made me turn my head toward my parents. I looked at them in a way I'd never done before; in fact, I was studying them. They had individually begun quietly to count the kids. When they both reached the number six, they looked at each other and broke into wide smiles. This is the precise moment that my life stopped being so abstract, and I could, at age nine, assign it meaning. I understood, right then and there, that for the rest of my life my notion of home would have nothing to do with the house.

We had no electricity or running water for nearly six months. The typhoon had swept away our baby pictures. We ate out of cans and washed ourselves and our clothes in a river

MIDLIFE'S A BITCH . . . OR IS IT?

I will admit that I strayed from my destiny in my adulthood. I left the island to attend college in Chicago. Like most kids who danced to Madonna in high school, I combined rebellion with a fervor to get rich fast. Rather than going to medical or law school, I broke my parents' hearts and worked in the food business, where I met Jenny, a celebrated Chicago chef. We married, opened our own restaurant, and made money. Like that of most working folks in the early '90s, our consumerism was greatly influenced by Ms. You-Know-Who. We built the big house in the country, planted the forty varieties of peonies, and so on. I spent a good part of the decade learning how to cook, entertain, build houses and gardens, shop for antiques, throw weddings, hire and fire landscapers and florists — a veritable lifestyle whirlwind. The restaurant was successful, we owned real estate, ours was a magazine-cover existence. I believed for a short while that we had everything.

Then I suffered a seizure on February 12, 1998, smack in the middle of dinner service in the restaurant. I went unconscious for several minutes and had an out-of-body experience. From somewhere above, I looked down at the world, my town, my block, and the restaurant. I was looking for the source of an unbearable, bloodcurdling scream that was interrupting my otherwise pleasant trip to the other side. Eventually I noticed that the screaming was coming from a stranger lying on the dining-room floor. At first I didn't recognize him, so I descended closer and realized in an instant that it was me. I woke up.

It was one of those incidents that was both inexplicable and physiologically inconsequential, but it traumatized me enough that I spent a few months assessing my life. I realized that despite my so-called success, I'd actually become an outsider again, this time in my own home. It was decorated with someone else's ideas, its rooms were plotted by the architect, we entertained the way you were "supposed to." I would freak out if one of the planters near the pool wasn't as lush as the others and would run to the nursery to fill it before friends came over for dinner. My wife and I would spend our precious free time running to this tag sale and that, looking through someone else's garbage in the hope of finding a platter to add to the many others we didn't use. It was, quite frankly, madness. I rescued

myself and in doing so embarked on my "lifestyle career," as some may call it. It's my life's mission, really.

I took the name Dan Ho, to honor my birth name. I asked myself, what could possibly be a worse lot than Dumb-dumb? Cockroach? Idiot? Murderer? Whore? Ah, Whore, of course! Reduced to Ho, it seemed entirely appropriate for someone in the media. I was the first to accuse myself of being hungry for a soapbox, the first to laugh at my funny name. Still, it is my sincerest desire that Dan Ho will one day mean all the things that my father's name means.

That's it. Today, who I am inside makes the style decisions; I am, in fact, my aesthetic. This is exactly as it should be for everyone.

INSPIRING THE SPIRIT

The practical problem with the philosophy "Your spirit is your style" is inspiration. What happens when your spirit is low, when your outlook is bleak? If you don't feel good inside, how's that supposed to look outside?

Here's what I believe. I assure you it is true. Human beings, you and I, wish only to belong. In this life, we want love; in the afterlife, we want to be somewhere specific, no matter how abstract the concept of the afterlife is. When we talk about living today, it's reduced to color, texture, taste, and cost. That's just wrong.

Family. Friends. Love. These will provide the sense of belonging we all desire. Keep these things close, and style will be bountiful. You'll see.

CHAPTER TWO

THE FIVE ELEMENTS OF *style*

Over time, I have developed something I call SLAVE, which is a quick, easy, yes-or-no style test. It is an acronym based on what I consider the five elements of style; however, I just love that the word *slave* accurately warns of what happens when we pursue perfection and buy into all that domestic diva caca. Plus, if anyone's going to slave over anything, it better damn well have some payoff of meaningful significance.

the five elements are:

1. SINGULARITY.
How original or different is the object?

2. LEGACY.
Is the object good enough to share or pass on?

3. ADAPTABILITY. Are your life and the object mutually compatible "as is"?

4. VALUE.
Does the object have a time and/or monetary advantage?

5. EMOTION.
Can you identify your personal resonance with the object?

If you get a yes answer to at least three elements, you're approaching *gai* — true style. Anything less is iffy.

THE SLAVE TEST

A QUICK GLANCE

✔ **SINGULARITY**

✔ **LEGACY**

✔ **ADAPTABILITY**

✔ **VALUE**

✔ **EMOTION**

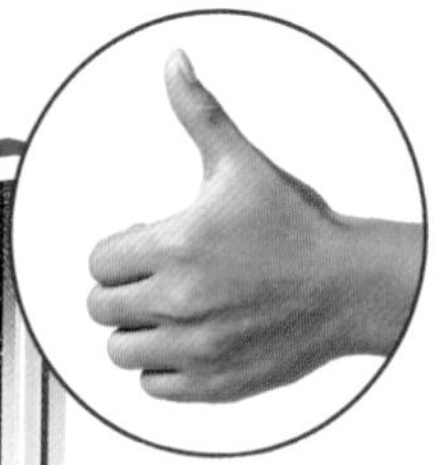

THIS IS STYLE.

These elementary-school class photos from the 1960s and 1970s are charming framed in either an inexpensive modern glass frame or an heirloom sterling silver Tiffany frame. Neither screams "moment!" — they are adaptable to any decor. No extra time or money was spent on matte board or mounting supplies — the photos were simply placed askew inside the frames to great effect.

✗ SINGULARITY

✗ LEGACY

✗ ADAPTABILITY

✗ VALUE

✗ EMOTION

THIS IS NOT STYLE.

These frames and this shelf possess zero singularity and adaptability. They're the kind of thing you'd sell at a garage sale in a few years. A black contemporary frame tends to look best in a neutral room with lots of neutral tones, and you'd be hard-pressed to pull off this look if it was mounted over graphic wallpaper. Truthfully, these frames were designed for mindless decorating; you could put any image in them and not change their boring, soulless effect.

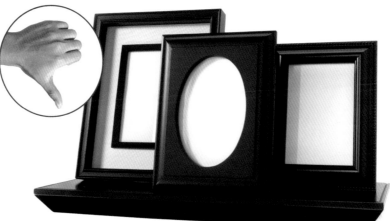

Singular is a term commonly used by geophysicists and rocket scientists to describe things like atoms, which are the smallest units of matter. The greatest scientific minds alive generally agree that all matter is made up of atoms — ain't nothing smaller; this is why they're singular.

Similarly, biologists say that a process is singular when nothing like it happens anywhere else in the universe, such as cell division. As far as we know, life exists only on earth, and one of

SINGULARITY

STYLE ELEMENT #1

IS IT ONE OF A KIND?

life's singular phenomena is that cells divide to create and sustain it.

In our day-to-day lives within and about our homes, gardens, and times of leisure and celebration, singularity holds a less scientific definition. Simply look around your house or apartment. That film wrap in your kitchen? Not singular; everyone uses it. Those cotton jersey sheets on your bed? Not singular, at least not since the daytime talk queen declared her love for them several years ago. A bazillion candles all over the place that are supposed to inspire romance and ambiance? Not singular, sorry.

Singularity of style is a tangible level of originality — for example, a one-of-a-kind lamp. But it's also the way you do things that's dif-

A bazillion candles all over the place? Not singular, sorry.

ferent from the norm. Let's say you wear only huge, round, black-framed eyeglasses, which is what the late fashion editrix Carrie Donovan did (you may recall her from the early Old Navy commercials). Even though you can get similar owl goggles anywhere, there aren't many gals walking around with them on, are there? Again, singularity can be manifested by (1) an object or (2) how you do things. Either way, a level of originality has to be there; at the very least, neither the object nor the action ought to be so popular that it falls into a type or category.

Clearly, you and I cannot live our lives ensuring that every object we own or every domestic ritual we undertake is an outright original. Tradition is an equally important element of style, as you'll read in a few pages. But singularity is not excluded by it.

Did you put away Grandmother's afghan because it was kind of ugly and didn't match your sofa? It's singular — take it out! If you mix and match things that weren't intended to be mixed and matched, that's pretty damn original. And if next Christmas you buy a better bottle of wine instead of giving cheaper wine in one of those velvet wine bags, you, my friend, will have done something pretty singular in the realm of hostess gifts. (What the heck do you do with a wine bag, anyway?)

ORIGINALITY OF ACTION.
The Shaker-style table is common. You can buy a veneered version at a flea market for the price of a movie ticket or purchase an antique or a new reproduction for hundreds more. The ubiquitous rubber ducky retails for around $7. You can have style with very little money.

THERE'S NATIVE AMERICAN JEWELRY, THEN THERE'S BEADWORK BY THE PENOBSCOT NATION OF MAINE AND NOVA SCOTIA. I like to collect it and when I'm in the mood to put on a piece of jewelry (which is rare) I commit to the idea of adorning myself with something handmade and scarce.

LEGACY, NO! Fake, mass-produced, rustic elegance is as dead as its components. As a style element, this pricey wreath holds absolutely no legacy.

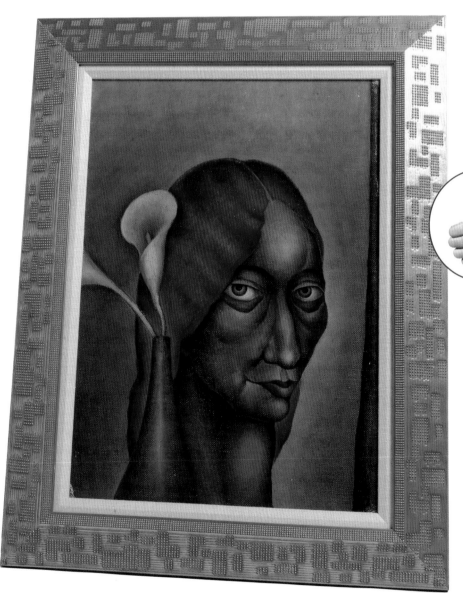

LEGACY, YES! This early-twentieth-century portrait by Swedish painter Karl Nelson is framed in a contemporary Braille-patterned frame. Its purchase price was less than a year's worth of weekly long-stemmed roses, which pale next to it as a style statement.

In the 1990s, when I was busy tending my three-acre garden, I'd spend money like it was going out of style. I'd buy trees that cost thousands of dollars. I was never satisfied to find just one variety of fern; I'd have to have a whole damn collection. There was a time when hostas — those sturdy, leafy, shade-loving mamas — were either the plain green variety or variegated white with a bit of curl to the leaf. Well, I don't know exactly when the hosta explosion occurred, but before I knew it, I was spending a ton of cash on giant blue ones, on teeny-tiny specimens, on some that had puckered seersucker leaves — who knows what else. Never mind the flagstone paths, the raised beds, the irrigation costs to plant them.

We sold that house a few years ago, but as I think about that garden today and consider all the blood, sweat, desire, and hope that I poured into it, I can get sad knowing that I wasn't able to pass some part of it on to my family or friends. The buyer was resolute that I was not to dig up or divide the plantings. He

If your style begins and ends with you, who's going to care? Worse, who will benefit?

was smart — they cost damn near what the swimming pool did.

When you have true style, it is, in fact, something to admire. It is part of your own personal legacy. It is therefore important that some part of it holds the ability to be shared, to be passed on, to be of use to others. If your style begins and ends with you, who's going to care? Worse, who will benefit?

LEGACY
STYLE ELEMENT #2
THE PASS-IT-ON FACTOR

Turn on any home show on cable television that involves remodeling a bathroom or a kitchen. Invariably, the host will make reference to the home being the single most important investment one will make in a lifetime. Therefore, to retain and increase the investment's value, you have to remodel an existing bathroom or kitchen or add on to it. Yet none of those hosts will venture into supposing why tending to the value of that investment is so important.

Is it so that at the end of your days, you can have it sold, and the more equity it yields, the bigger and more elaborate the obelisk at your grave site? Of course not! Come on. We're better than that. Have some *gai*.

Are you trying too hard? Check yourself. We all know what that looks like, and it ain't pretty. Isn't this the truth? When people have style, the things they do seem effortless. They are able to go through their day seamlessly; the stops and starts aren't apparent. There are no such things as crises in their world; the fact is, few things have more élan than when people keep their cool while everything seems to be out of place.

ADAPTABILITY
STYLE ELEMENT #3
THE EVERYDAY FIT

Consider cooking. Professional chef or not, a cook who has *gai* will use the knife and cutting board she has out to mince garlic. It's efficient; all you need is a sharp blade and a cutting surface. Conversely, the cook prone to junking up his kitchen with gadgets will stop what he's doing to dig for the garlic press. He'll ignore that he's already got the cutting board and knife out — he needs them anyway to clean the clove for the garlic press. If he can't find the garlic press, then watch out, it could be a crisis.

What other uses does a garlic press have? It can't be used to press almonds or apples or boiled eggs. It can't even help mash vitamins for your morning protein shake. Garlic presses simply are not adaptable; they actually interrupt the flow of cooking.

Life is full of interruptive clutter. If you buy a throw pillow that "inspires" you to redo your living room so it looks good in it, that pillow is a trap.

Asparagus steamers are just about the dumbest things ever invented, and I am sad to say that I used to own a fine specimen purchased from a very upscale retailer. For one thing, I rarely steam asparagus; I prefer them grilled or sautéed. The few times I did get around to using it, I'd have to dust it off and wash it first and then have to put it away when I was done. It wasn't suited to my everyday life, using it was awkward, and it was nonsense the moment I brought it home.

Life is full of interruptive clutter. Garden centers sell tulip bulb planters — if you have a shovel, you don't need one. Home stores sell soap-making kits, but for the price of the kit and supplies, you can buy really nice soap. If you buy a throw pillow that "inspires" you to redo your living room so it looks good in it, that pillow is a trap. Worse, it makes you lose appreciation for what you already have, and already paid for.

If your stuff ain't adaptable, it ain't giving you style.

ADAPTABLE. This dollar-store steamer likely fits in any pot you already own and works for preparing anything from asparagus to fish, or for steaming hamburger buns. It also collapses and stores nicely.

NOT ADAPTABLE. This expensive Mexican *mocajete* is often marketed as the "ultimate" tool for making authentic guacamole. Not true. It's a pain to store and scratches surfaces. And who's anybody kidding? If you're not an authentic Mexican cook, use the spice grinder or a plain bowl that you already have.

SO YOU WANT A ROMANTIC AMBIANCE?

Doesn't it seem preposterous to add scraping candle wax off the bathtub to the already-dreaded task of cleaning the bathroom? Even though votive candles are cheap, they burn very quickly and, quite frankly, are contrived.

If it's romance you're after, put a drop or two of your favorite perfume in your bath, turn the lights down low, and put on a little music. Sure, the perfume is expensive, but the effect and ease are pure style.

Value, as an element of style, is fluid, because what something is worth to a sampling of individuals isn't always reducible to the same constant. Some can say, for example, that a new Bentley is a steal at $150,000, while others fail to see any value in a waterfront acre lot priced at one dollar. "What's it worth to you?" rarely gets the same answer twice. Of course, if you can get the same thing for less money, by all means, go for it.

I find that the question of worth is answered by a couple of things: money cost (up front) and/or aggravation cost (hidden).

MONEY COST

It's really important that you spend your hard-earned money on things that are well made, especially these days, as cost and quality don't necessarily reflect each other. You can go to your local chain bed-and-bath store, for example, to purchase a nylon exfoliating sponge and easily spend upward of ten dollars, yet I can guarantee you that it will not match the quality and versatility of a nylon massage towel that any Chinatown merchant sells for less than two dollars. Sheets and pillowcases are another example. If you catch a really good

"What's it worth to you?" rarely gets the same answer twice.

sale or are an adept online shopper, you can score a really high thread count for less than what you'd pay in-store for lesser-quality sheets.

VALUE
STYLE ELEMENT #4
THE QUALITY EXCHANGE

AGGRAVATION COST

They say that growing your own vegetables saves you money. Oh yeah? Who cares when you can drive to your local farm stand and pick up tomatoes for less effort than you'd spend catalogue-shopping for seeds. And who's kidding anybody? Your antibug budget will eclipse what you'd spend on the tomatoes you'll actually eat.

I refuse to believe that rational people really believe stripping paint and inhaling caustic fumes is the best way to spend their precious free time. Yet, in the name of value, people will poke through junk shops and garage sales for this very job, hoping to find a dresser or a set of chairs on the cheap. If you spend time and money looking for old painted furniture, then you ought to love it as is. Don't spend all that energy looking for something you wish to change. You will be ahead time and money if you go for what you wanted in the first place.

Looking perfect does not equal qualitative gain. I often cite the example of candles providing instant, inexpensive ambiance in the bathroom. For what purpose? Romance? Mood lighting? Aroma? Considering that we already despise cleaning our bathrooms, doesn't it seem preposterous to add scraping candle wax off

---

EMOTION
STYLE ELEMENT #5
WHY IT MATTERS

---

the tub to scrubbing the toilet? Screw the candles, even if they don't cost much. You want romance? Buy a La Perla thong. Ambient lighting the goal? Crystal chandelier on a rheostat. Aroma? Chanel No. 5, baby, eau de parfum!

If legacy is the *future* element of true style, then emotion opens a window onto a rich and important *past*. It is the history that exists between you and the object.

If only for superficiality's sake, using things that have been passed on to you provides a stylish edge to your home and person. As unstylish as it is to prepare the Easter ham the way Grandma did it — even if you're dying to serve a newfound recipe of organic pork loin stuffed with wild mushrooms — it's vital to your spirit, your sense of belonging, which is ultimately style. If you must eat off all-white china, go to any cheap restaurant, and that'll cure you. But if you have a relative's china in a box somewhere, convinced that those dishes and spoons that have nurtured your family or friends aren't "your style," then, my friend, you wouldn't know style if it broke your nose.

Fortunately, matchy-matchy has been a fashion no-no for quite some time, even among the domestic divas and divos, so it's socially acceptable to use old with new. Use the stuff that already exists in your family first, before you go out antiquing for someone else's discarded wares. It doesn't matter if the family stuff is Wedgwood or grocery-store stamp-traded cups or old McDonald's glass mugs with Mayor McCheese. Mix it up, and keep in touch with your roots.

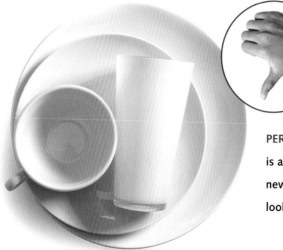

PERFECTLY STOIC. Matched all-white dinnerware is as sterile as an infirmary. If you're investing in new plates, at least go for something that doesn't look completely void of personality.

STYLE IS IMPERFECT. None of these pieces match, they don't stack, and they aren't entirely dishwasher safe. But they mean something because they have a personal history.

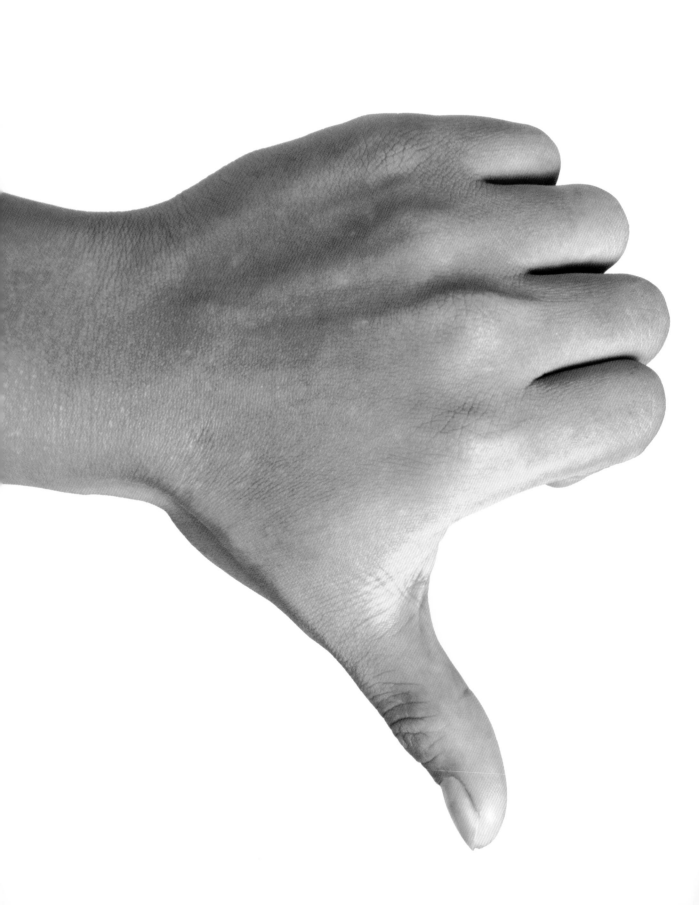

CHAPTER THREE

THE SEVEN ENSLAVING

H ard-and-fast rules are nonsense, especially when it comes to how we live in our homes, tend to our gardens, cook our meals, and socialize. Allow me this opportunity to point out a few outright lies that require some serious redressing.

MYTH 1: focal points are important

Don't get me wrong. I believe that rooms (and events) should have focus, but the point should not be to reduce a room to what the attention-hog designers and decorators call the focal point. Every time I hear this term, I cringe, I know right then and there that whoever said it needs to be rescued. A focal point, by nature, is an optical illusion, which, in a word, is fake.

Shelter has a dual function, the first being protection, which translates stylistically to coziness or intimacy. **You can be neither cozy nor intimate in a room where the color, furniture, and accessories have been intentionally placed so that a mirror, a painting, or a fireplace demands your attention.** Many window companies and contractors have gotten rich from home owners wanting to turn an expansive view into a focal point. But the window-treatment sector has benefited far more from shades, blinds, and drapes — things that cover up the so-called focal point.

Shelter's second role is utility, otherwise known as function. I know someone who made the focal point of his dining room a lovely rustic fireplace. So that it could be viewed from every point

Ultimately, you and your family should be the focal point of your room.

in the room and beyond, he bought a glass dining table and the most awful uncomfortable iron chairs, whose grillwork you could see through. In this case, the focal point completely interrupted the function of the dining room, which was to dine. No one wanted to endure the painful chairs.

You don't have to go out of your way to show things off. My friend should have just been grateful for the nice fireplace. It would have been a stylish surprise at dinner, instead of the joke it became. Ultimately, you and your family should be the focal point of your room. If something inanimate is, you've got no *gai*.

MYTH 2:
color, pattern, and texture should be unified

Designers, decorators, wedding planners, and style divas all want us to think that colors must coordinate, as if two colors' placement on the color wheel is the be-all-and-end-all on the subject. That if you have taupe walls, the carpet had better not be hot pink. Why the heck not? Or that if you have a painting, you ought to try to "pull" the colors in it throughout the room. That's just semicooked cable-babble.

Similarly, pattern and texture don't have to be clones of each other. A bride's bouquet absolutely does not have to match the flowers on the cake; she should, in fact, be as singular as possible. A new all-leather living-room set is stark and cold, but a leather chair next to a silk couch is cool. And how good is a chocolate cream pie if the crust is as creamy as the filling?

You may very well love all things white, Lucite, and spotless. You may look good, but you are missing the important style elements of adaptability and legacy.

MYTH 3:
buying in bulk saves money

It doesn't matter if it's food, pillows, or grass seed — you simply cannot save money if you're wasting it on bulk buys you don't use.

If you have a little pillow to cover and discover that the fabric you want is cheaper by the bolt than by the yard, don't buy the bolt. You'll make the pillow, yes; but then you're stuck dealing with the rest of it — where to store it, moving your things to accommodate it. All that takes time, and time is money.

Buy only what you need. You'll save money and aggravation.

MYTH 4:
the easier, the better

Not necessarily. The queen of England's homes are maintenance behemoths, but she doesn't have to worry too much about attending to matters herself. Her life is easy. Pity that she may have go to blow her nose once in a while (but I'm sure she doesn't have to grab the Kleenex herself). On the other hand, a guy with a simple landscape of turf easily gets overwhelmed by cutting the grass, edging it, fertilizing, irrigating, and reseeding. It's all relative; however, true style isn't a disposable thing, which means some level of maintenance is required. (How else can it have legacy?)

You may have to, as I do, hand wash a couple of plates every now and then. I don't have two sets of flatware — the good silver is used every day, which means every now and then I have to polish it. A good wool sweater may need hand washing, while the ten crappy ones you saw on the extremely melodramatic makeover show require only machine washing and drying.

Measure the sum of maintenance in your day-to-day life; seek balance and adaptability. Remember, style is knowing what matters the most, and being a pop-up cleaning-wipe queen isn't. When you maintain the objects that surround you, you understand why they're important by being reminded of their personal resonance.

MYTH 5:
you should always be ready for drop-in guests

No, you shouldn't, unless you're running a bed-and-breakfast. Even then, ever hear of reservations?

Hospitality is not having a guest room and bath, outfitted with a fluffy five-star bathrobe and a basket of mini-toiletries. Nor is it stocking a pantry that allows you to throw together

Style is not an act of accumulation.

It is serious editing.

a fabulous meal at a moment's notice, or allocating and maintaining a "reading area" somewhere specifically for reading books.

Hospitality is generosity with your personal time and space, the ability to go with the flow. If you've got the domestic-diva guest room set up, so what? Maybe you should take in a boarder.

MYTH 6:
you can always use more storage space

Imagine our lives if we owned only the dishes and glassware we really use, the Tupperware was filled and washed constantly, the clothes that came off our backs went right into laundry or dry cleaning and then back on again. Think of all the money we'd save. Think of how much smarter our homes would be. Think of the style possibilities. I don't know about you, but kitchen cabinets — don't care if they're made from cashmere and gold — are just boxes to hold stuff.

Dream of how much better, how benevolent and stylish, we'd all be if we bought one pair of really fabulous shoes a season, rather than three or ten. Even if we didn't save money,

we'd save on aggravation. We've become consumers who ooh and aah over closets, toilets, and sinks. Come on. We should be enthralled by things that matter.

The more storage you have, the less style you have. I'm sorry, it's just the truth. It smacks of greediness and slovenliness; it won't kill anyone to buy toilet paper in four-pack rolls instead of packages the size of a washing machine.

MYTH 7:
fresh is always better

The most gorgeous shrimp cocktail you ever had was frozen on board the ship that netted it. So was all the expensive bluefin tuna sashimi anyone has recently had. Dried pasta is far more reliable than fresh and, in my opinion, better-tasting.

I've seen fake branches of silk dogwood blooms that look better than the actual cut branches in big, expensive fresh arrangements. Imitation, old, not-so-perfect has its own appeal. If you've ever drunk a deliciously heady glass of Sauternes, you might know that vintners refer to it as "the noble rot." New and "authentic" isn't always better; anyone who tells you otherwise cares too much that his or her vanilla is pure.

the 3-things test

Imagine if your house burned down or was completely lost in a flood or hurricane. Perhaps you lost your luggage with your best clothes. These events are kind of scary to think about, but as we all know, they happen.

Would people still recognize you for who you are? Would you be lost and insecure without all your stuff?

As you read this book, I want you to think about all the things that define your style, and then reduce them to three items according to the guidelines below:

1. SOMETHING THAT WAS FREE.

2. SOMETHING THAT COST UNDER $100.

3. SOMETHING THAT WAS AT THE TOP RANGE OF YOUR BUDGET WHEN YOU BOUGHT IT.

PART II

HOW TO CHOW

CHAPTER FOUR

THE DISCERNING *cook*

T he chasm between what we know and what we do is most evident in what designers like to call "dream kitchens." Stainless-steel and granite countertops notwithstanding, we have become a nation of overstimulated, overinformed cooks who have veered far from the essence of good cooking. In the name of design, we actually believe that propane or gas is delicious — or else most of us would be grilling over flavorful wood charcoal in our humble Webers. For the sake of culinary bling, we're boiling dried pasta made who knows when in order to enjoy in-season, local tomatoes. We really believe that perfect fried chicken includes a buttermilk marinade, a goopy flour-egg-flour dip process, and a "proper" frying pan.

You know how you can always pick out tourists in New York City? The camera around the neck, the sweatpants, the gawking, the bag full of tchotchkes? Behold their culinary counterpart: the cook in the American dream kitchen, where spices have their own drawer, lemons have their own zester, and the purpose of life is death by chocolate. Don't get me wrong, I love a good Chocolate Dump Cake; however, dream cookin' in this country is an embarrassing mishmash of redundant, sometimes bad information.

It's downright garish to have a professional kitchen if you don't feed at least thirty people a day. Contrary to designer babble, a kitchen with limitless culinary possibilities is not style. Limits, in fact, are very *gai*.

be a mindful cook, not a mindless one

CURB VARIETY BY EATING SEASONALLY

There is no such thing as year-round summer. Even in places as hot and tropical as Guam, mangoes grow only certain times of the year. Ripe strawberries shouldn't be available year-round. Because it is a staple in sushi restaurants, we dismiss the fact that tuna don't really migrate along the gulfs of Mexico and Maine to feed and spawn, but they do. To be brutally honest, were chefs more attuned to this, fish stocks wouldn't be as dangerously depleted as they are now, and customers, in turn, would simply have to order something else.

On a basic level, we understand this, which is why things like Crock-Pots and food dehydrators mostly gather dust. We make stews in cooler months and, if inclined, naturally preserve food toward the end of the season — but we don't know what to do with these appliances the rest of the year.

REINFORCE AND RECOMMIT TO YOUR INDIGENOUS HOME COOKING

If you're not from Calcutta, stick to mashed potatoes instead of stocking up on the spices and ingredients for *kavurma;* they're better at the Indian restaurant, anyway. What in the world are you doing with a tortilla press? Get thee to your local bodega or Mexican restaurant for some real ones.

Cooking at home should not be about replicating fabulous international recipes with all the attendant aspects. Heck, professional kitchens don't even have "proper" pots — ever peek behind the scenes at a busy bistro? You aren't going to find Le Creuset, All-Clad, or other so-called professional-grade ware. Rather, the kitchen will more than likely use cheap commercial aluminum frying pans that they hurl across the line into a dirty bus tub.

DON'T GO CHASING WATER BATHS

In other words, stick to what you're best at. It's okay to be limited to one style of cooking or a few dishes. No one expected Julia Child to cook Swahili, you know what I mean? It's okay to be singular and limited.

I personally prefer to bake a whole chicken one way. I split it, taking the backbone out, then I rub it with salt, a little pepper, and olive oil — that's it. I don't care that there are a million ways to cook and flavor it. I don't have a Bubba Gump complex with the bird. And when people come over for chicken, I'm not making coq au vin.

EAT LESS

That's right, we eat way too much in this country. If we ate right-sized portions, pasta bowls, hot chocolate mugs, and refrigerators wouldn't be so huge. We wouldn't kid ourselves that pantries are so important, and that confusion of plastic leftover containers would not junk up our cabinets, our kitchens, and our lives.

the *gai* way to cook

Cooking is the application of effort and energy to maximize the flavor and nutritional quality of food. Really, the essential point of cooking a steak is to boost its native flavor and bring it to temperature. In this sense, a marinade doesn't necessarily assist the essential flavor of a swordfish steak; it tends rather to cover up its intrinsic charms. Similarly, grilling the fish doesn't bring out its flavor, either; all that does is make it taste like the smoldering ash of wood.

THE COOK'S FIVE

My philosophy is that your spirit is your style, and the same goes for food. The more style a dish of salmon has, the more we taste the salmon and the less we taste the "recipe." This is age-old thinking; I certainly did not invent "less is more." But after years in the restaurant business, eating my way from coast to coast and through some parts of the world, I can say with certainty that besides heat and water, cooking at its best is facilitated by these five basic ingredients:

- SALT
- PEPPER (PIQUANT, I.E., BLACK PEPPER, CAYENNE, ETC.)
- FAT
- AROMATICS (ONION, GARLIC, FRESH OR DRIED HERBS)
- ACID (CITRUS JUICE, VINEGAR, BEER, WINE)

METHOD MATCHING

Contrary to popular chefese, cooking methods and food groups cannot be crisscrossed and taste wonderful. Grilled fruit and grilled Caesar salad, for example, are contrived nonsense. Lettuce is best raw, thank you.

	RAW	FRY	SAUTÉ	BAKE	BROIL	GRILL
Leaf vegetables	Yes	–	Yes	–	–	–
Root vegetables	–	Yes	–	Yes	–	–
Fruit	Yes	–	Yes	Yes	–	–
Seafood	Yes	Yes	Yes	–	Yes	–
Poultry	–	Yes	Yes	Yes	Yes	Yes, if whole
Beef	–	–	Yes	–	Yes	Yes, in big cuts
Pork	–	–	Yes	Yes	–	–
Lamb	–	–	Yes	–	Yes	Yes, in big cuts

Essentially, there are just a few ideal methods for each type of food. Sautéing is really the best method for most, and grilling serves poultry, beef, and lamb best if whole pieces or large cuts are cooked. If you are conscious of these limited methods (and the Cook's Five), then you hone real cooking instinct — you won't have to rely on sensationalized, irrelevant cooking trends.

Raw:

Fruits, leafy vegetables, and seafood

QUARTER GUACAMOLE

4 firm and ripe avocados, quartered lengthwise,
spooned from skins
2 medium tomatoes, firm and ripe, cut in eighths
1 tablespoon chopped green onion
1 tablespoon chopped fresh cilantro
zest of ½ lime
juice of 1 lime
salt and pepper to taste
1 avocado pit, to keep color
optional: 1 teaspoon minced jalapeño or serrano pepper

Use a light touch to combine all the ingredients, keeping
the avocado as whole as possible. Chill until ready to
serve.

SERVES 4 TO 6 AS A SIDE SALAD

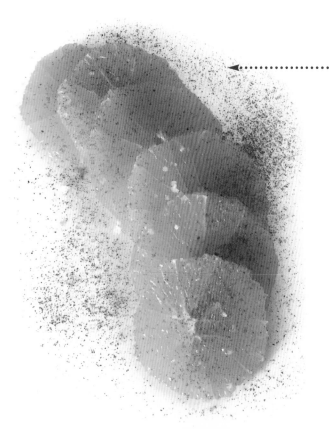

SALTED & SPICED RAW FRUIT

Any juicy fresh fruit is delicious with a pinch of sea or
kosher salt and a tiny bit of spice. Try some of these com-
binations.

Watermelon	Salt
Cantaloupe	Salt and cumin
Oranges (shown)	Salt and paprika
Papaya	Salt and cayenne
Pears	Salt and cinnamon or anise

Fry:

Root vegetables, seafood, and poultry

PARSNIP FRIES

3 cups light olive oil, for frying
2 pounds parsnips, cleaned but not peeled, cut into fries
salt
pepper
fresh thyme

Heat olive oil in skillet until approximately 350° or a test fry cooks evenly. Fry parsnips — be sure not to crowd them in pan. Cook until evenly browned, about 3 minutes.

Remove and drain on paper towels. Season with salt, pepper, and chopped fresh thyme.

Serve immediately.

SERVES 4

FRIED SHELL-ON SHRIMP WITH BASIL

20 pieces shell-on shrimp, size 16–20
¼ cup olive oil, for frying
20 whole leaves fresh basil
sea or kosher salt

1. CLEAN

Incise top of shrimp, cutting through shell to devein. Do not remove shells or feet. If heads are not intact, trim top end of shrimp to remove any discolored flesh. Rinse and drain on kitchen towel or strainer for 5 minutes.

2. FRY

Fry in heated oil for approximately 2 minutes, turning regularly for even cooking. When the shrimp is done, add basil and cook for 30 seconds, until wilted. Salt just before serving.

SERVES 4 TO 6

Sauté:

Anything except root vegetables

CHINESE LONG BEANS WITH GARLIC

2 pounds fresh Chinese long beans
4 tablespoons vegetable oil
4 cloves garlic, sliced thinly
salt
pepper

Wash long beans, snap off ends, and trim to 4-inch lengths.

In a large pan, heat vegetable oil and cook garlic until fragrant. Add long beans and sauté quickly (about 2–3 minutes) until beans are bright green and slightly browned at the edges but still crisp. Season with salt and pepper.

Serve immediately.

SERVES 4 TO 6

FRESH SAUSAGES WITH ONION

6 fresh sausages, such as Italian, chicken, etc.
2 tablespoons olive oil
2 large onions, sliced thickly into 1-inch wedges
1 teaspoon sea or kosher salt
½ teaspoon cracked pepper
¼ cup beer
¼ cup fresh parsley, roughly chopped

In a large pan, evenly sauté sausages in oil over medium heat for 8 minutes. Remove and set aside. Turn heat to medium-high, and sauté onions in same pan. Add salt and pepper and cook until translucent. Add beer, scraping bottom of pan, then add cooked sausages. Cook for 10 minutes, until onions are brown and internal temperature of sausages reaches 160°. Transfer to platter, and top with parsley.

SERVES 4 TO 6

Bake:

Root vegetables, fruit, poultry, and pork

ORANGE WITH OVEN-DRIED SKINS AND CHOCOLATE

peeled orange segments
chocolate

Carefully peel and segment oranges so that skin remains unpunctured and excess pith is removed.

Place slices on cookie sheet and bake in 200° oven for 5–7 minutes. Remove and let cool.

Serve either dipped in chocolate or plain with chocolate.

SWEET POTATO WEDGES WITH GARLIC

3 large sweet potatoes, scrubbed and sliced lengthwise into wedges
20 whole garlic cloves, in skin
2 teaspoons sea or kosher salt
½ teaspoon cracked pepper
3 tablespoons olive oil

1. BAKE

Combine all ingredients in shallow dish in 350° oven for 1 hour. Sweet potatoes should be crispy and soft, and garlic cloves should mash when pressed.

2. SERVE

Serve on large platter. Encourage guests to squeeze soft garlic onto potato wedges or pieces of bread.

SERVES 6 TO 8

Broil:

Seafood, poultry, beef, and lamb

SALMON TEMPLADO

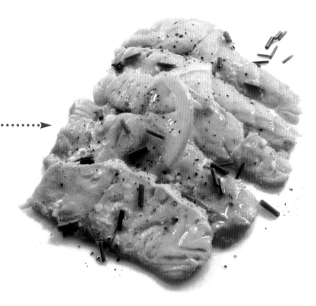

20 thin slices raw salmon fillet
2 tablespoons extra virgin olive oil
1 lemon
sea or kosher salt
cracked pepper
fresh chives or scallions, minced

1. PREPARE PLATES

On four ovenproof plates, divide slices of salmon evenly as shown. Drizzle with small amount of olive oil to coat. Turn broiler on high.

2. BROIL

Place plates under broiler for 10–20 seconds, watching closely so that salmon just turns pink and begins to brown at edges. Remove plates.

3. DRESS AND SERVE

Dress plates evenly with extra virgin olive oil, fresh-squeezed lemon juice, salt, cracked pepper, and chives or scallions. Serve immediately.

SERVES 4

TWICE-HAMMERED LAMB CHOPS

juice of 1 lemon
1 ounce Pernod or ouzo
4 tablespoons olive oil
2 tablespoons fresh rosemary, chopped
8 lamb chops
salt
pepper

Combine lemon juice, liqueur, olive oil, and rosemary in shallow baking pan. Mix well.

Hammer loin portion of chops by covering with plastic wrap, then gently but firmly flatten by pounding with rolling pin or mallet. Place chops in baking pan and smear with lemon-oil-rosemary mix. Season with salt and pepper.

Place chops under broiler for 2–3 minutes on each side, and cook until chops are medium-rare or done. Remove chops to platter, then place pan over medium burner. With fork, quickly scrape the pan juices into a loose sauce.

Drizzle chops with sauce and garnish with lemon peel and rosemary.

SERVES 4

Grill:

Whole pieces of poultry, beef, and lamb

SIMPLE LEMONY CORNISH HENS

juice of 4 lemons
⅓ cup olive oil
4 Cornish hens
12 strong bamboo skewers
salt
pepper

Mix lemon juice and olive oil and set aside.

Wash and pat dry Cornish hens, skewering each as shown (through the wing, the back, and the legs). This will give them stability on the grill.

Slice hens diagonally across breast and legs in shallow cuts and pour lemon oil over them. Rub well, seasoning all sides with salt and pepper. Let rest for 20 minutes. Don't marinade for much longer than 1 hour.

Place hens on medium grill with even heat, breast-side down first. Cook for 8–10 minutes, being careful not to turn until skin is well-done. Turn over and cook for an additional 8–10 minutes, until temperature between thigh and breast is 165°. Remove and let rest for 3–5 minutes. Do not grill for more than 20 minutes — internal temperature can be achieved in a 350° oven.

Add a pinch more salt and pepper just before serving.

SERVES 4

UN-BBQ BEEF BRISKET

4-to-6-pound beef brisket, untrimmed (as much fat on it as possible)
salt, for rubbing
olive oil, for rubbing
pepper

1. CLEAN
Vigorously rub brisket with salt on all sides, then rinse thoroughly. Pat dry on kitchen towels, rub with olive oil, and allow to rest.

2. GRILL
Place whole brisket on grill over indirect heat (push coals to side) and cook covered for 30 minutes on each side. After an hour, wrap brisket loosely in heavy foil and continue cooking for an hour and a half.

3. FINISH
Remove brisket from foil and place directly on grill for 15 minutes on each side or until internal temperature reaches 140°. Remove from heat and let rest for 20 minutes.

4. TRIM AND SERVE
Trim any residual fat from brisket and slice thinly. Arrange on platter and salt and pepper lightly just before serving.

dressing, but in fact (sssshhh), many restaurants and caterers use it as an efficient base for reliable sauces.

Here are a couple of my mayonnaise concoctions. Come up with some of your own, using another base such as butter or sour cream. The idea is to have something that's singular to your cooking style, while being versatile with what you've got.

CONDIMENTS

As much as we can hope our guests enjoy the broiled lamb as we prepared it, not having the A.1. steak sauce they love diminishes the meal and the gathering experience. So you should have this kind of stuff on hand, but don't go overboard and junk up your pantry. Have one kind of hot sauce, one kind of relish, and so on. Try not to turn your refrigerator doors into a sticky confusion of forgotten jars and bottles.

THE MAYONNAISE TRICK

You gotta love old-fashioned mayonnaise. Not only does it serve as the base for classic tartar sauce and beloved Great-Aunt June's Russian

LEMON CAPER SAUCE

SERVE WITH SEAFOOD, POULTRY, VEGETABLES

2 cups mayonnaise
2 tablespoons capers
juice of 2 lemons
zest of 1 lemon
salt
ground white pepper

Combine and stir. Serve chilled.

GARLIC CHILI DIPPING SAUCE

SERVE WITH FRIED OR BAKED CHICKEN AND FISH, VEGETABLES, SANDWICHES

1 cup mayonnaise
1–2 tablespoons Thai chili sauce
1 tablespoon chopped scallions
1 teaspoon ground fresh ginger

Combine and stir. Serve chilled.

pairing food with wine, etc.

As much as I dislike using food as theater in a social interaction — it's a complete entertaining cop-out — I shrink more at the overanalysis of pairing wine with food. I've been to too many dinner parties where the host waxes ad nauseam about the wine he's pouring, and everyone looks like a silly nut swirling and chewing the wine, offering the obligatory exclamations. I said earlier in the chapter that professional kitchens aren't the hallmark of a home kitchen. Similarly, if you've got a wine collection at home that befits a restaurant, you may be a tad bit greedy, if not gluttonous.

A dinner can be perfectly satisfying, indeed memorable, without the fruit of the vine. Water never goes out of style, and a good steak pairs inexplicably well with a cold, dry martini. In fact, some food goes better with beer, particularly Asian (Japanese, Thai, Vietnamese, and Chinese) or aromatic and nutty Middle Eastern food. It's really pedantic when chefs on television suggest serving western wines with something like pad Thai. In most cases I understand the flavor match. Gewürztraminer, for example, works with the sweet/sour/salty Chinese flavors; and (duh!) a sashimi of delicate white fish will obviously not argue with Chardonnay. But my point is, Asian food is better accompanied by easily found Asian beers or other traditional spirits such as sake.

That said, not all beer has to be microbrewed and unique. Not all tea has to be procured from the finest merchant and steeped loose in special pots. It's only food, it's just drink. Lighten up and don't be such a show-off. Remember, style is perceptible. It doesn't need talking points.

CHAPTER FIVE

PLATE IT *forward*

You and I know people who are sushiphiles. They go out and buy square Japanese stoneware to serve the sushi they make at home, even though they already own perfectly good plates. An admission: in my own home are two or three Spanish *cazuelas,* which are shallow, round earthenware pans for paella. However, this house comes by them honestly — Jenny was a chef at a tapas restaurant for many years, so she's got an emotional attachment to them. She uses them to bake fruit crisps and as planters for paperwhites. But if she hadn't protested, they'd have been dog bowls.

We can't fill up our lives with what I call "one-trick ponies." A Japanese square plate purchased for the exclusive use of sushi is nonsense. But if you allow yourself to expand its use as a soap dish or a change tray, then you've got *gai.*

As you've probably surmised, the limited methods that maximize the flavor and nutritional value of food types rationally yield a limited possibility of accoutrement. For example (I reiterate here), the delicate process of sautéing preserves the intrinsic flavor of fish far better than the harsher grilling method. Therefore, you don't need the friggin' fish attachment for the grill or a whole fish flipper and all of the other crap that is developed and marketed for the well-intentioned, if misguided, consumer.

Home cooking and exquisite cuisine are not mutually exclusive; home- and restaurant-style, however, are. Eating at home is, and should be, different.

FAMILY STYLE VERSUS COURSING

To me, the success of a meal is directly related to the number of plates used: the more plates you use to serve it, the less *gai* it's got. Using appetizer plates, bread plates, salad plates, chargers, and umpteen utensils is a formality that does not belong at home unless you have servants who can bus and serve. I feel so sorry for the blokes who get suckered in by the makeover quintet guys to design a candlelit dinner with four courses for their wives or girlfriends who have "suffered" living with them. These dudes can hardly trim their nose hairs, never mind coursing an overblown dinner. A far more sensual affair would be a restaurant dinner or a picnic with champagne — let's be real, people.

Instead of wasting energy plating up food on different dinnerware, running back and forth from the table to the kitchen sink or dishwasher, set a table for the entire night. Serve family style.

KNIVES AND BEYOND

Do you know why getting thrown into the deep end of a pool has worked for more student swimmers than most would care to fathom? It's because the body and mind are capable of solving problems without expert input. You don't need to go to chef school to learn how to use a knife properly. Simply use it over and over, and the technique will come to you naturally.

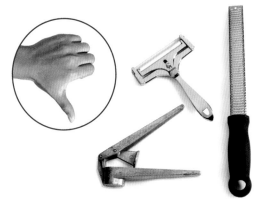

All this gadgetry is just junk.

Consider all that one good knife gets you and the crap it spares.

A whisk gets you cake, whipped cream, and custard — you don't need an electric mixer. A low oven dries out fruit just as well as a fancy food dehydrator does. Again, style isn't hauling out special equipment to do something. Style is using what you've got and displaying ease that you've earned by instinct.

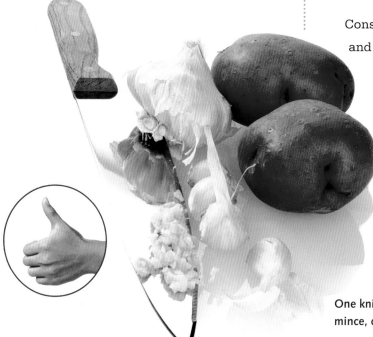

One knife and practiced technique will peel, zest, mince, chop, flatten, chiffonade, dice, etc.

Style is easy. Newspaper is used as a disposable tablecloth, glass pie plates are placed over leaves you pick from your yard, cold bottles of beer are ready to drink, and a stick of butter in its wax-paper wrapping is ready to rub on corn on the cob.

Style does not necessarily require an iron. For the effort, go out to a nice restaurant and relax at a nice table set for two. Individual salt and pepper cellars are such a waste! Is fresh-cracked pepper from a reliable pepper mill not in vogue anymore? I didn't get the memo.

What's more memorable,
you or what you serve?
Think about it.

CHAPTER SIX

PANTRIES, PLASTIC, AND

storage

My mom, bless her, endures my endless ribbing about her typhoon-resistant pantry. Well, it really isn't a physical pantry, per se. There is no room in her home dedicated to canned goods, beans, tabletop propane stoves, paper plates, and rice; that is, if you don't count the mini-Costco at one end of the dining room, hidden behind a folding screen, and the five-thousand-gallon water tank on a concrete square right outside her bedroom window. Long before the reality show *Survivor* was even a twinkle in any network exec's eye, she and my dad used to hop on puddle jumpers to the nearby island of Palau to buy fresh fish, which she would then distribute to my siblings and me wherever we may have been at the time — Spain, Chicago . . . wherever.

Was this excessive? By the standards of many, sure. I haven't mentioned what they'd pay for express mail from Guam! But is it style? Yes, it is. This is not nepotism here — I assure you that my family's state of *gai* is naturally, and regularly, overthrown. By contrast, my late mother-in-law, Jeanne, was reared fairly affluently but in years following the Great Depression. She could never abide by mother's excesses, yet her home and cooking had *gai* nonetheless.

Mingle, mingle! It is perfectly all right and downright eye-catching to store your food with your dishes. We waste far too much sleep and resources on storage ideas that are nothing more than obsessive-compulsive-disorder traps.

THE EMPTINESS OF BULK STORAGE

You and I have no rational reasons to hoard food in the manner that designers and TV chefs imply that we should. As much as the lifestyle industry proclaims we are a culture that values a quasi-gentrified life, no matter how rolling the meadow or severe the chic, the truth of the matter is that we don't value it enough that we completely commit to it. We've all got to work; we're working more than our parents did.

And let's just be honest about the hoarding mentality that the perfect pantry supports. Food isn't fresher — how can it be if you buy what you think you might use next year? Tastes change — you may not want to eat it next year. You don't really save time going to the market — you're always going to need fresh milk, fruit, vegetables, and toilet paper, anyway.

American women marvel at their European counterparts. How can they wear high heels and walk on cobblestones? How come they're not fat, yet they eat carbs and sugar all day? They smoke, so they can't be gym rats. Aren't their towns charming with the old buildings, narrow streets, and balconies?

Well, therein lies part of the answer: the goldfish grows according to the size of its bowl. The late Dr. Atkins is a veritable deity in our country, yet obesity is on the rise. We continue to be prone to weight-controlled diabetes, though a monthly gym membership can cost less than the price of two packs of ciga-

Food isn't fresher — how can it be if you buy what you think you might use next year?

rettes in some towns. If our cities lack a nostalgic bustling charm, it's because we are loath to live in the same apartments or homes we may have grown up in — we just don't do that. But they do it in France.

Now, I suppose if, like the stylish Europeans, I opted to live in my parents' home, I'd come by the bulk-buying thing honestly. Instead, I pursued the American dream and that to-die-for pantry not expecting that it would be a hall of mirrors. You don't need it, you never needed it, it's got no style. If you have one now, consider turning it into a deluxe kennel for your dog or cat. Or use it to store all the dishes and pots you don't use, the clothes you won't wear again, and other things you'll discover are crap as you read this book. Call it your Legacy Room, and regularly invite family, friends, and charity organizations to loot it.

Refute the storage-space myth. Your focus should be on fresher food, versatility, and going to the market more often (which burns calories).

ZIP AND SEAL VERSUS FILM AND FOIL

Look, if you've got rolls of foil and film wrap, then you don't need plastic bags that zip and lock. And if you eat yogurt, buy olives at the deli, pig out on the guiltless pleasures of Cool Whip, you've been wasting your money on those space-eating gremlins known as "leftover ware."

Few things are more futile than leftover Thanksgiving turkey in a zip-and-lock bag. In the name of time and space saving, the bagged-up turkey goes into the fridge, only to be assaulted two hours later. It comes out of said bag onto a clean cutting board or plate so it can be sliced for a sandwich. This happens over and over, dirtying up clean plates, knives,

and cutting boards. The bag itself becomes greasy and gross; its ability to zip or lock fades. When at last the bird is devoured, what do we do? We wash the damn bag, hoping in vain to restore it to some greaseless resemblance of utility, and turn it upside down on the faucet or kitchen counter, mucking things up. Oy. Vey. We would have ended up saving far more energy, resources, and time had we just stuck the bird on a plate with a piece of foil.

You obtain the same nonsense with the matchy-matchy set of plastic containers, some

My pantry is at once a laundry room, pot rack, vanity, and utility room. It is in what used to be a hallway off the kitchen.

Manufacturer labels are interesting to look at if you can get past the need to reorganize what's already organized.

of which are now semidisposable, which makes no sense to me. You can easily place extra soup in a coffee mug covered with film wrap. As I said, it's stylin' to get multiple uses out of things you own. One-trick ponies are for the birds.

RE-CONTAINERING

Behold the even more time-wasteful, zero-*gai* nonsense known as display storage. I understand that at some point in history this method worked for the home dweller; however, the bubonic plague is long past. Even during these horrible times of anthrax and dirty bombs, there is no rational or stylish reason to take food out of its well-designed, sani-

tary bag or box only to stick it into something else. I don't buy the ants and bugs reason, because re-containering doesn't get rid of the ants and bugs in the first place. And if humidity is the problem, steal an extra produce bag at the store, and slip it over the bag of flour — you're obviously buying too much in the first place.

Don't get suckered in by designer types who extol the virtues of "merchandising" opportunities — in other words, the ingredients function as contemporary objets d'art. Truthfully, commercial packaging is better art.

There's a reason Andy Warhol is considered an artist. Can you imagine if he had put his Brillo pads in a cutesy canister set?

Behold the even more time-wasteful, zero-*gai* nonsense known as display storage. There is no rational reason to take food out of its well-designed bag or box only to stick it into something else.

CHAPTER SEVEN

ENTERTAINING! EMPHASIS
entertain

I have long been titillated by the overlooked details of food; and by that I mean the aspects of eating and entertaining that are epic and metaphorical yet deeply and quietly poignant. I love that the word *companion* can be literally defined as "one with whom you break bread." It packs so much more punch than *friend* or even *best friend.* Our contemporary usage of it implies intimacy, recognition, and presence. *Salt* is cool that way, too. The engaging history writer Mark Kurlansky's book *Salt* chronicles its savory history, pointing out the breadth of its meaning to us — literally life and death. We at once aspire to be "the salt of the earth," yet we strive to retire from our "salt mines" as soon as humanly possible. Would truffles hold such office?

You'll understand that the first time I heard a television design guru proclaim that a dream kitchen is the "soul of the home," I just about expelled a green worm. Come on, it may very well have cost the same as the house itself, but when things are reduced to the important stuff, it's got the same plumbing, refrigeration, and heat as a mobile home. While I love the power of words to mean more, **the soul of any home is within its inhabitants, plain and simple.**

Since this irrational beatification of the kitchen, entertaining style has itself become a competitive spectator sport. When I'm invited to a friend's house for dinner, especially after a long, difficult week, I have no interest in watching my hostess cook or helping to slice a baguette into croutons for the bruschetta or tapenade. Forget it! That's not hospitality — it's slave labor. I'd rather pay for dinner with the money I spent the week earning, thank you.

There's more style in a bowl of Cheetos and a cold Budweiser than in your goat cheese salad and appletini.

Here are a few ways to keep entertaining at home stylish and real.

BE AS COOKED AS YOU CAN BE

The food you intend to serve ought to be nearly ready to eat when your guests arrive. Salads should be prepared and chilled, the table should be set, and the wine glasses should be out. This is not to be misconstrued as perfection; really, it's to keep gathering to gathering. Not hunting or preparing. Fuss over something else.

This also applies to grilling. The grill is not a conversation piece; watching food cook and smoke is about as exciting as laundering smoke-smelling clothes. By the time your guests arrive, your grill should be turned off and the food cooked to the point where it can hold in a warm oven for serving.

KEEP COCKTAILS SIMPLE

Offer booze on the rocks, mixed, or straight up. If you're serving margaritas and other foofy drinks, do the messy work beforehand, and keep them cold in the fridge or freezer.

PLAN A CONVERSATION

If you're hosting a friend of a friend, find out from the friend about the person he or she is bringing. If an old cousin or a spouse's colleague is stopping by, think about what the guest is all about, and base a conversation on that. At all costs, try to avoid the talk turning to the food itself, and for heaven's sake, resist giving a tour of the house. Is that the best you've got? Have some *gai!*

BOARD THE PETS IF YOU MUST

I am a devoted daddy to two dogs, yet I'd be a horrible host if my guests spent the evening wiping drool off their clothing. Your evening shouldn't be spent saying "No!" and "Down!" Keeping your four-legged family members away, if it's necessary, is hospitable.

IF YOU DON'T HAVE KIDS, YOU DON'T HAVE TO BE KID-FRIENDLY

In other words, you don't have to be a beacon of social etiquette if your guests feel it's okay for their little ones to forgo learning social skills early. When I was in the restaurant business, I really dug (and so did the waitstaff) the kids who were behaved and ate off the menu. But when a parent special-ordered pasta with butter or grilled cheese with fries for their kids, we all took bets on how long it'd take a neighboring table to complain about the unruly brats. Of course, if you're cool with all that, fine, but be warned: the most inhospitable thing you can do is maintain a bald-faced lie to your guests. (No, I don't mind that your kid's giving me a migraine.) Be honest.

the potluck

I get tingly when I think of an Amish barn raising. A community of friends and family comes together, bringing whatever they've got to help someone out, and in doing so, they strengthen the character — indeed, the style — of the community. Potlucks get to me the same way.

There are two approaches to a potluck. First is potluck by assignment, where the host plans a menu and decides who is bringing what. Typically, you reserve preparing the main course for yourself, but hey, if sister Suzie makes a better roast and wants to bring it, enjoy the break! I would encourage you, however, to supply all of the beverages. The second way — my favorite — is potluck by surprise, meaning you give someone a general category and leave it up to them. Saying "Surprise me" allows you stylishly to accept beverages, since you won't be asking your guests for specific wines, let's say, to match the planned menu of a potluck by assignment.

Potlucks are gatherings of the highest social order. I mean, they're so damn civilized but in an organic, natural, very human way. They are also much less stressful and offer the host the opportunity to gussy up and concentrate on other things besides cooking the entire meal.

theme dinners

Except on the rarest occasions where the host cook is extraordinarily gifted in cross-cultural cuisine, keep food that is not indigenous off the list of theme possibilities. As I've implied, if you're as Irish as they come and haven't had much experience cooking Thai, don't send out invitations for "An Evening in Bangkok at My House." Trust me on this one, you'll score a knockout doing what you do best, even if it's chili dogs.

Still, I adore wit — everyone does. Why not use a timely news story as the theme for your dinner? Say the inspiration is Lance Armstrong's seventh Tour de France win. You could do improbable pairings of soul food and French wines — you know, banana cream pie with vanilla wafer crust and Chateau d'Yquem? Or flip it and reverse it, yo: grape soda with Perigord truffles. Well . . . you know what I mean.

the wisdom of takeout

If you've got a really good pizza place near you, let them do the cooking. Some of the best dinners I've ever been to have been delivered from local takeout places. Samosas, curried lamb, and naan (the tandoori bread that is easily reheated in a hot, dry frying pan) from the Indian place, a platter of *maki* rolls from the sushi joint — why not? Short of actually dining out, you can enjoy a lot of good food at home without filling up your pantry with exotic ingredients you may hardly ever use.

Gather menus from your favorite places, paper-clip them together, and stick the bunch right next to your spice rack. Allow yourself the freedom to open up your cupboards and say, "Tonight I think I'll make love instead."

the foxy host

Finally, it's important to look your best when you entertain at home. I realize that this seems to come out of left field; in fact, it smacks of some kind of how-to for socialites, doesn't it? It is vital that your best pearls and diamonds greet your guests, especially if you must endure the indignity of answering the door yourself. Uh-huh. Right. But I'm being serious.

We live in a world where all that we are tends to be compartmentalized. At work we're one thing, at the gym we're different, at home we're something and someone else. Lately, at-home personal style means schlumpy. It's not so cool that we reserve being engaging and well turned out for the anonymous public, instead of for our family and friends, who are most deserving of our best. Admittedly, I remain inspired by my parents, who cared to fuss, but I am absolutely certain that we all remember our mothers and fathers looking good when they invited company over. Today it is far too easy to put on a

"couture" jogging suit and shapeless designer shmata that offers only its price tag as a poor excuse for social grace and personal style.

In the beginning of this book I said that if friends, family, and love are your priority, style will follow. Even if you're having a backyard picnic, don your bling, do your hair, and step into your finest soles. Years from now few will care to remember the food and furniture, but mark my word, your kindness and hospitality will be enveloped by a cherished vision of your allure.

If you have a pizza oven in your home, I feel sorry for you. Leave it to the pizza people.

PART III

HOW TO COZY

CHAPTER EIGHT

THE *living room*

Call me a dinosaur, but I love a good old-fashioned living room. By that I mean the one room in the house where the matching pair of armchairs is supposed to live. It's kind of fallen out of fashion; in fact, design gurus have all but stripped it of its name in favor of *living space.* In some cases, especially in McMansions, they've just plain disappeared, morphing with the kitchen and the dining room into a wide-open superroom that makes it difficult to complain about the cook behind her back or watch television without thinking about the dishes. Yet the drive for coziness remains, resulting in the designer prescription for "sitting areas" scattered in bedrooms and bathrooms. This is nonsense. Let's be honest: if you're in a bathroom, there's really only one place where you'll be doing the sitting, and it ain't gonna be on the chaise.

It is so easy to get distracted when looking for inspiration to create a living room; it rarely occurs to most of us that the space itself is essentially an expansion of what happens when two chairs come together. We all know that even a sofa is not that necessary to achieve a comfortable room; four large easy chairs around a coffee table are plenty of decor and comfort to do the job. In the Gospel of Saint Matthew are the words "Where two or three are gathered . . . I am there"; and if you use the reference as a purely literal one, it can be a more fertile design seed than color, texture, and theme. **The ability of two people to sit together in tranquility surrounded by objects that represent a family's personal culture is inspiring stuff.**

mixing furniture

Jerry Hall, in an über-*gai* moment, pretty much summed up the mission of sofas and chairs: that they be worn and shabby when she drops dead. True, her actual words (I paraphrased here) were captured on the set of her reality TV series, where male contestants vied for the once-in-a-lifetime chance of being her boy toy, but who cares? Wisdom is wisdom; it isn't franchised exclusively to the likes of Deepak Chopra.

Fabulousness is a highly personal science, so administering themes and decorating rules is futile. Really, the most lucid way to get style is to have an ideology you can apply in any situation. I call mine the High-Low.

The High-Low is the deliberate compromise of decor so that you obtain true uncompromising style. It ensures that any room passes the SLAVE test (see chapter 2): that it has Singularity, Legacy, Adaptability, Value, and Emotion. It's a brake that keeps you from going overboard and out of *gai*. It's, at its most basic level, letting go.

By the way, letting go as a concept has articulated singular style throughout time. When Elizabeth I of England let go of the "princesses must marry" norm of her day, she went down in history as the Virgin Queen and by doing so branded herself hip enough to lend her cachet to theater and English furniture. Coco Chanel could have easily disappeared into obscurity had she not decided in the 1930s that comfort (rather than the postwar ideal of layered and fitted) was important and that costume jewelry and cotton jersey were just as fashionable as silk charmeuse. She let go. The rest is history. The advantages of letting go aren't limited to famous people; we see it every day. Don't we all have friends who met their significant others on days when they didn't care to look their best? Letting go rocks.

the high-low in real life

STEP 1. GATHER THE OPPOSITES

	HIGH	LOW
Chair pad	Matching	Mismatched
Blankets	Cashmere	Afghan
Artwork	Centered	Off center
Lighting	Halogen	Incandescent

STEP 2. DEEMPHASIZE THE OBVIOUS

If you've got a view, good for you, but turn your back to it. If you're in a period house or apartment, veer toward contemporary, and vice versa. Don't gild the lily; go for irony and anachronism.

STEP 3. ENCLOSE WITH SYMMETRY

Again, decorators scream about "opening up" and "letting light in." Light is good, of course; however, living rooms (any rooms, really) should be defined and cozy. It makes no sense to diminish the coziness of one room in order to "tie in" other rooms of the house. It's better to have one good statement than a bunch of half-assed ones.

Enclosure is accomplished by symmetry. Our bodies find comfort in symmetry — they are, in fact, symmetrical. As kids, we long for a mother on one side, a father on the other; yin seeks yang. Visual symmetry goes a long way in translating comfort. All it is, really, is equidistance. This can be as simple as two tables (not necessarily matching) on either side of a sofa or two chairs on either side of a table.

Sure, it's a fireplace, but who cares? Books spill out of the bookcase onto the marble mantel. I don't need to have the obligatory pair of candlesticks, and photos, to turn the fireplace into an inefficient focal point.

The easiest, most efficient way to establish symmetry is with a rug.

walls, floors, and windows

A simple rule for walls, floors, and windows is the "I Don't Wanna See It" rule. If your floor is hardwood, okay, we get it already. It doesn't have to be so shiny and so visually expansive that it hogs all the attention. Likewise, if you love lilac so much that you would paint your walls with it, it shouldn't be the dominant feature in the room. A few years ago, when vertical blinds were the rage, you walked into a room, and hello! You couldn't miss them.

One single element in your room should not be the inspiration for how the rest of it evolves. Life doesn't work that way, and neither does true style.

ABOVE: I suppose I could dwell on the fact that the molding throughout my house is the original 1865 mahogany, but I don't. The house is dark and very Victorian. I didn't want to draw any more attention to it and ordered skinny white miniblinds from the local curtain shop.

LEFT: I don't like the word *eclectic* because it hints at a lack of discipline. In fact, my living room has undergone my strict SLAVE test. Style is knowing why things matter to you. It's not a visual set of rules.

Neutral is overrated. The wallpaper is purple leather, the molding is mahogany, and the carpet is a semi-shag. I didn't want any of the three elements to be more noticeable than the others, and instead all three strong elements together possess balance.

comfort

There's a lot to this word, we so toss it around lightly, and our concept of it seems to be limited to how good our backs and butts feel on a chair or how neutral a color scheme is in that it mimics the supposedly restful realities that lifestyle-catalogue covers imply. But if you really think about it, comfort implies a few other things:

BODY CONSCIOUSNESS

Seating to crawl into and cozy up in is a wonderful thing, indeed; however, our bodies aren't always so cozy-able. If, for instance, the important people in your life have back problems or are simply older, a firm chair with sturdy, grippable handles must have precedence over a Le Corbusier piece. They can't comfortably spring up from a dream of deep-seated, down-filled cushions. On the flip side, I can't imagine being comfortable in a sleek Lucite chair. I doubt that most people would.

SAFETY

Candles may spark and pose a fire hazard. Sharp edges on tables must be considered if flimsy rugs are placed on the floor without proper backing. If you have pets, you must ensure that your plants or rocks in bowls don't interest them enough to cause an unfortunate incident. Are your electrical outlets overloaded? Can they really accommodate all the mood lighting and audio equipment you've got in the room? Check your home for safety. It's absolutely worth it.

USABILITY

Can people really drink red wine on your couch or rug without your having a secret anxiety attack? Do you put photo albums or boxes out and not really want people to look at them? If all of this stuff goes on in your head, you won't be comfortable, and neither will anyone else. This absolutely drives me nuts: a glass table I can't put a drink on, a floor on which shoes aren't allowed.

art

There is a huge difference between art and decorative objects, and it's one that has been largely ignored by TV decorators and designers. They freely use the word *art* as though a surfboard sawed lengthwise and stuck on a wall were the same as a charcoal study of a nude executed by an important American artist. I've actually heard kitchen designers claim that ventilation hoods and cabinet knobs and handles are the art of a kitchen. I completely disagree. While art can certainly be decorative, its function is to impose its singularity onto everyday life. It should stop the eye and the thinking process and not ever be displayed in order to blend or "tie in" with a room. That said, a well-placed piece of art can elevate any room, whether it be professionally decorated or in a mobile-home park, into the realm of true style (see photo, right).

Real estate agents like to say that every house has a buyer; and the same applies to art. We can't all own van Gogh's *Irises,* nor can

we all claim a fabulous five-dollar wood-block print found in a dusty attic somewhere. If art is daunting to the novice buyer, it's because the art-owner relationship is one of a kind; searching for and learning about the art you are ultimately destined to own is not unlike a series of first dates. It's damn awkward.

That's right, I'm saying that you can successfully decorate with art while forgetting about color and subject matter.

Appointing your living room and home with art will take time. I know people who buy furniture to decorate the house they're planning to buy. Don't — decor is easy. Style's pace is the daily grind, and so you ought to think about the art first.

ESTABLISHING A COLLECTION

The art in a room tends to get very matchy-matchy if it is collected based on its visual aspects alone. Don't get me wrong, looks must appeal to you, but you can go about growing an interesting and stylish collection by taking a decidedly unvisual approach. That's right, I'm saying that you can successfully decorate with art while forgetting about color and subject matter.

BODY OF WORK

If an artist appeals to you enough to invest in more of his or her work, expand your scope of interest by looking at earlier or later pieces. Works in a series tend to feel the same, and your collection might be less interesting if you limit your pieces to one series. It is a guarantee that if, say, you collected three paintings from the same artist created at different times over several years, instead of from a set window of time, the group will be far more varied.

TIME FRAME AND CONTEMPORARIES

What else was going on in the world when your painting was created, or what inspired its subject matter? Who else was making art at the time? If your piece's artist is old or dead, find out what school he or she went to, or try to find out where his or her work may have been shown. Then see who else was there, and seek their work out.

TECHNIQUE

Sometimes limiting yourself to a particular technique allows your collection to have personality. For example, encaustic paintings are sealed with hot wax; this technique has been employed by artists seemingly since the beginning of time. They're not all of Byzantine or classic representational style; encaustic is used with modern abstracts as well. You can build a collection of encaustic paintings spanning many artists and many eras, and it can have great style.

BEYOND THE GALLERY: FINDING ART

I've seen some of the worst nonsense in galleries; so while they are the most logical places to conduct your first dates with art, be careful. But if a gallery is showing a retrospective of an artist's work, meaning a representative collection of work the artist has done over time, then it's a sign that the gallery owner or director can be a good source of information.

Besides galleries, I find that these are great sources of information and inspiration:

ART SCHOOLS

Go to the galleries at your local college of arts, and pay close attention to the senior and faculty shows.

MUSEUMS

Believe it or not, museums have what they consider junk, too. There is sometimes a dusty room with stuff that they might be willing to part with.

ARTIST SPACES

In most metropolitan areas, there are buildings that rent out studio spaces to artists. See if you can't charm your way into the halls to see what's up.

GOVERNMENT

As hard as it is to believe, most state governments have a staffer or two knowledgeable about state art programs. The good news is that grants tend to go to recognized artists, so in some measure, the state has good taste.

Give them a call, and see what shows or spaces they are sponsoring or if they fund an ongoing archive of local works and collections.

FRAME SHOPS

Find the edgiest frame store in your area, and go take a peek. You might be lucky enough to see what they're working on. Feel free to ask them who's doing what, and they might know of artist shows well in advance of when they go up.

ART RESTORERS

These experts are few and far between, but if you've got them in your area, they're likely to be in the know about who's got what, who's selling what, and where they are.

LOCAL MEDIA

Read the local art critics and culture-oriented newspapers for features and schedules of art-related events.

FRAMES AND HANGING

Frames should never match; in fact, the frames should never cost more than the artwork, except on the rare occasion when you get a really good buy. It's better to spend the money on the actual piece than on the transitory frame.

You only need to employ two very simple methods to create harmony with a varied collection of art and frames. First, hang gallery-style as shown. Second, space the edges of the frames equally so that the disparate styles achieve a pleasing sense of belonging in the grid of space that separates them.

accessories

ACCENT PILLOWS

You should never have more than one accent pillow per human spine in the room. For example, if you have a sofa that seats three, it should never have more than three accent pillows. Otherwise it's just irrelevant junk, and the money is better spent on a better couch or mortgage principal.

WINDOW TREATMENT

What looks good on TV doesn't necessarily look good in person, and this is never more true than with window treatments. Be very careful of the do-it-yourself bug. Don't haul out a circular saw, a cordless drill, a staple gun, and batting if all you're trying to achieve is a valance with clean lines. If it's simple you want, stick with blinds, shades, or simple curtains. Conversely, if elaborate quasi-rococo is what you pine for, success is easier to achieve with your imagination and a glue gun than with a pissy decorating diva on retainer.

PLANTS AND FLOWERS

I personally prefer live greenery to cut flowers; however, if you disagree (and you probably should), try to keep your arrangement "types" the same according to your favorite two or three vases.

High-Low Test: Can you tell what on the facing page is the least expensive? The most expensive? It doesn't matter, but for the record the lace tablecloth from Camariñas, Spain, is the priciest element.

TABLES AND TABLECLOTHS

You can forgo fabric on your windows, but do try to use tablecloths on your accent-room tables. They are instantly cozy and high-style, especially if they're old hand-me-downs.

ACCENT LIGHTING

Candles don't set a mood, people do, so keep nonsense candlelit ambiance to a minimum. A simple rheostat cleanly does the job of "mood" lighting. Lamps should never match unless they're of good quality (legacy-worthy) or have been inherited, in which case they should be cherished no matter what their resale value is.

TCHOTCHKES

If it's something from your past, by all means set it out, but put it in an unexpected place. Groups of tchotchkes or collectibles work well on tabletops or shelves; scattering them throughout dilutes the emotional impact.

ELECTRONICS

Decorator babble states that computers, stereos, and televisions ought to be hidden from sight in living rooms. I don't completely agree. If you have so much equipment that a behemoth armoire hogs the attention of the room, that's dumb. Since we're constantly upgrading our computers, the next time you get one, try a super-duper laptop or a flat-screen PC or Mac, and load your music into it. Televisions in living rooms shouldn't be larger than the largest chair in the room.

CHAPTER NINE

THE *bedroom*

S ome gurus say that they can judge people by what kind of shoes they're wearing, which is not entirely evil. Humans are, after all, imperfect, and I myself consider my own shoes an important part of who I am inside. Still, I think that there are more accurate means to getting inside the head of someone. For me, that's by looking at their bedroom. Here's what I think. **Your bedroom reflects your level of generosity. If it is not inviting, it's because you probably aren't.** Even the Three Bears invited Goldilocks to stay for dinner, am I right?

We throw sheets on the guest bed that we wouldn't put on ours. We use leftover, halfhearted effort to pretend we're hosts of the highest caliber by giving our loved ones pillows that we wouldn't sleep on ourselves. Making your guest comfortable is the key to being a good host — please don't overlook how important this is.

So there's the big style secret for bedrooms: by giving to others, you give to yourself. This is style — this is *gai.*

What, then, does generosity look like? The truth is, it can look like anything; individual taste will dictate. Ultimately generosity involves parting with that which is valuable to you. Taking a cue from *worth,* the elements of generosity are the four Ws: weight, wind, warmth, and water.

weight

ENTRANCES AND EXITS

A bedroom should absolutely feel as though it is the safest place in the home. I love a view as much as the next person; however, if the feeling of protection is compromised by a wall of glass that looks out onto a foreboding ocean, then it diminishes the bedroom's ability to be a place of rest and restoration.

WINDOWS

By and large, any means of ingress and egress (ways a person can get into or out of the bedroom) are the largest consideration of weight. Windows, as I mentioned, are one means. If your bedroom window is in a first-floor urban alley, it makes complete sense to secure it as much as possible (or have your landlord do the honors).

DOORS

Bedroom doors rarely get as much attention as they deserve, which is slightly baffling from a decorating standpoint, as they are a very large interior feature. I really consider my bedroom door as the lid to the jewelry box. It's heavy, it closes with a solid click of the door handle, and it's as beautiful as any door in the house.

TRANSITIONS

Beyond the door, some attempt at a transition ought to be articulated in order to expand the difference between the rest of the home and your inner lair. Establishing this threshold can be as easy as placing an area rug just inside the bedroom door or, if you're thinking of remodeling, establishing what approximates a small foyer or hallway between the door and the main part of the bedroom. Although this is unusual, it is logical. When our front doors open right onto a sidewalk, we don't feel as safe from the street as we do when there's a front porch or stoop in between. The same holds true for bedrooms; a transition is extremely effective in giving weight and separation to the room.

THE BED

The bed should be the only piece of furniture that you can lie on. I say this because designers love to throw in chaise longues and "seating areas" in unnecessarily large rooms and call it style. It's just misinformation.

Indeed, the bed is the single piece of furniture that comes closest to boasting that it's the "soul of the home" (sorry, kitchen designers). You can eat, sit, work, make and have babies, and live and die in bed. It's all about the bed in the bedroom. If there's another piece of furniture that you can fall asleep on, all it's doing is lessening the necessary weight the bed should have.

OPPOSITE: You can't tell by looking down the hall where my bedroom is, and that's the point. It should be discreet and safe.

CONNECTIVITY

I don't subscribe to the glorious quasi-altruistic idea that televisions should be banned from the bedroom, that they rob you of the opportunity to read and connect with your spouse or yourself. My own dear mother refuses to put a phone line in her bedroom, and I say, "Ma! *Amanu y yomu gai?!*" (Where's your *gai?!*) Alas, I may be a dumb-dumb on this point, but it makes far more sense to me to fall asleep in front of the television while you're in bed than when you're on the couch.

Phones, laptops, televisions. If all parties are in agreement, use these as weight elements in your bedroom. You'll want to stay connected and informed.

LIFE

You really ought to have a plant or two in your bedroom — something that needs checking in the morning and at the end of the day. Plants give weight to a room, as well as reinforce a metaphor for life. They give oxygen and cause you to preen your lair with regularity. When you tend to the well-being of something else, it all comes back to you.

wind

Pass out the nitro to the design divas, 'cause we're hauling in the ceiling fans.

A bedroom must have air movement, and the more natural the better. Can anything be more restorative than a breeze? Really, think about it. We can all certainly recharge with

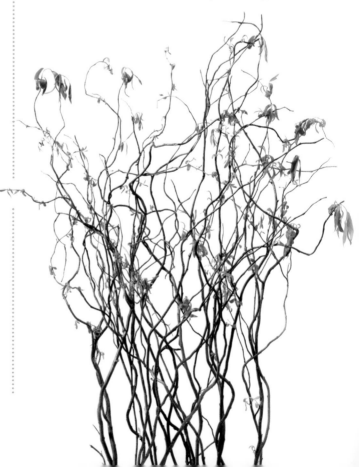

It really irks me that the goons on the makeover shows are so dismissive of the elemental necessity that is addressed by the ceiling fan.

sleep, food, or drink, but we're never quite as renewed as when a breath of wind embraces us. It really irks me that the goons on the makeover shows are so dismissive of the elemental necessity that is addressed by the maligned ceiling fan.

Obviously a floor or table fan is just as lovely, and neither is, of course, as effective as throwing your window open for the real thing. Be sure that your bedroom can benefit from the cleansing, living movement of air.

warmth

FLOOR

The most expensive hotel I ever stayed at had marble floors, which caused me to walk as if I had heel spurs. Your bedroom should have a warm and soft floor — like a nest. Put down some carpet, and on top of that throw down a nice rug or two. If you are remodeling, replace old carpet, if necessary, but resist keeping the floor bare. Carpets should have as thick a pile as you and your vacuum cleaner can manage.

WALLS

Any layer over the paint on your drywall or plaster adds warmth, so long as the surface isn't reflective. Mirrored walls give the impression that there are no walls, which seriously diminishes the feeling of being protected.

Similarly, stark bare walls in bedrooms don't feel restful; the magpie in us seeks the comfort and enclosure that relics and art provide.

HEATING

If you have the choice, insist that the bedroom have the best heating in the house. It's dumb if the great room and the dining room are hogging all the efficiencies of your ductwork, while you and your family lie shivering in your beds. Kitchens have ovens and stoves, living-room entertaining requires (in most cases) clothing, but when you sleep in your God-given skin, you ought to do so in warmth.

LIGHT

The bedroom should be well lit. You can achieve the warmth of varied light with lamps and overhead lights on rheostats.

LINENS

Beds should not be so difficult to turn down that you're encouraged just to sleep on top of the bedspread or duvet. The bed in one expensive hotel was so excruciatingly perfect that I had to help the maid get it ready to sleep in. Designers today love to pillow and bead a bed to death, disregarding the lovely pleasures of accessibility. Beds are not meant to be gazed upon as though they were the pillow aisle at Nordstrom. A warm bed isn't one you're afraid to mess up.

water

If you watched *Gunsmoke,* you might remember the water pitcher and bowl somewhere in the room at Miss Kitty's hotel. On or off film, people naturally keep water and bed together (think of the cool, damp cloth on a loved one's feverish head). Though out of fashion, water in the bedroom is not a new idea, but one that is terrifically adaptable to updates.

SINKS AND TUBS

Sinks and tubs are great in bedrooms; in fact, they are much more useful and natural than the newfangled seating areas in a corner of the room.

A simple sink and a mirror at one end of your bedroom are quite sensible. Designers say that they save time in the bathroom, but if that's the idea, shouldn't there be two toilets as well? Let's face it, if you're on the pot, there will be no line at the sink station.

The same holds true for fabulous tubs in dream baths. Why would anyone want to soak and be on the same eye level as the toilet? Wouldn't you rather be close to the bed so you can recover gloriously from your hot bath?

OPPOSITE: Instead of a sitting area in my bedroom, I have a soaking tub.

reliquary

Reliquaries are sacred spaces for religious or personal relics. Our homes abound with them even if we don't know it. The proverbial junk drawer is a reliquary, that one place where you throw things that are mismatched but too important to throw away. Dresser surfaces are another kind of reliquary, where deodorant is mixed with jewelry, money, keys, and a treasured photo of a loved one. In a shared bedroom, there are usually two reliquaries: his and hers, or any combination thereof.

The bedroom reliquary is a prime place to gather orphaned heirlooms such as plates or bowls, to organize change, jewelry, and so on. You don't need matchy-matchy Lucite boxes and impersonal baskets. Think of reliquaries as your own dynamic anthropology. They should be a snapshot of your past, present, and future.

linen tricks: mix, match, make do

We are fortunate to be consumers in the golden age of discount shopping. There are great deals to be had on bed linens, each sale better than the next. But linen stocks in this superdiscount world are unreliable. Fortunately, we've learned to mix and match, which, in and of itself, is very *gai*.

Still, the abundance can also lead to overload and waste, so here are a few tricks to keep crap to a minimum.

THE TRANS-SEASON BED SKIRT

I hate bed skirts; they're a prime example of a great idea turning into a bad solution. They're unreasonably expensive, they're flimsy, they hardly ever fit, and ironing them is a bitch. What if I told you that you didn't ever need to buy one again? Well, I'm telling you!

Simply use an off-season blanket or duvet to cover the box spring. An unused quilt makes a terrific bed skirt, as does a top sheet. As long as the piece is sized for the bed you have, just about anything will do (see below).

A simple knot at the corners fixes a too-generous drape, or simply turn it under and pin the corner to the inside for a sturdy, floor-skimming drape.

STEP 1: Take an off-season quilt or blanket sized to your box spring.

STEP 2: Drape evenly over the box spring.

STEP 3: Place mattress over it and dress.

STEP 4: Finish the bed.

STEP 1: Press king-size pillowcase.

STEP 2: Place pillow against the far end of pillowcase.

STEP 3: Tuck excess fabric inside case and to one side of pillow.

STEP 4: Crease new folded edge.

STEP 5: *Voilà!*

KING-SIZE FITS MOST

If you find a great king-size comforter on sale, it'll fit a queen or full bed as a luxuriously oversize duvet — go for it.

King-size pillowcases, which are always in abundance at great markdown, fit standard-size pillows with the easy fold-and-tuck technique shown above.

THE TURNED-DOWN FINISH

If you like a finished-looking bed but for some reason or another don't have the pillow shams or don't have the time and inclination for the rest of the dog-and-pony show, a simple, low-starch ironing of your pillowcases finishes a made bed in the most awesome way. No ironing of sheets (as if). A blanket over the top sheet, the duvet folded, and neat pillowcases — that's all you need. One ironing lasts between washes.

DARK HEAD TRICK

When pillowcases are a darker color than the rest of the mix-and-match sheets, you forget that they're mixed or matched. Your eye stops at the pillows and tricks your brain into thinking that everything below it is a set.

DOGS KNOT ALLOWED

If your dogs are allowed to sleep on the bed, it is impossible to keep the top surface clean without always changing or washing it — and who has that many duvets or comforters? A quick, no-sew, poly-fleece doggie throw is a great solution.

TWO-SIDED MIX-FRIENDLY DOGGIE BLANKET

1. **PIECES**
Purchase two 2.5-yard lengths of poly fleece (60 inches wide) in one or coordinating colors. Place one on top of the other.

2. **FRINGE**
On all edges, through both pieces of fleece, cut a 6-inch fringe. Space strips 1 inch apart.

KNOT **3.**
Tie the corresponding lengths of fringe in two successive knots.

WASH 'N' DRY
Toss into the laundry as often as necessary.

CHAPTER TEN

THE *bathroom*

I f I ever go down in history as a decorator type, I hope that I'll be distinguished as the guy who started the trend to make bathrooms smaller. I suppose it's a dubious honor given the mad rush to make everything huge, but I'll take it. Whatever you stand for in life, it has to mean something solid to someone else.

As far as I'm concerned, a bathroom's utility peaks at washing your person and flushing the toilet. Anything past that is a misguided waste of time and resources. A bathroom isn't great for storage, it makes a horrible home pharmacy, and it's a poor excuse for a beauty shop. As I pointed out in the previous chapter, it is no place to relax in a bath given the proximity to the commode and its attendant uses. Whoever coined the term *water closet* was spot on. Bathrooms needn't be more than that.

I find endless fascination in bathrooms on airplanes and trains; they are just so damn efficient. The coolest shower I ever took was in a sleeping car, where the showerhead was in the same tiny room that housed the toilet and the sink. **Designers and decorators go about bathrooms today as though our bodily functions were tea ceremonies and shaving were meditation.** No matter how opulent they become, none of us seriously wants to spend more time in a bathroom than is necessary; so it makes absolutely no sense to turn them into temples.

Do your thang 'n' get out, you know what I'm sayin'?

the difference between cleaning and beautifying

Cosmetics companies have long been clear about what separates clean and beautiful, which is why *skin care* is different from *color*. You rarely see cleansing products right alongside lipsticks, do you? Pond's Cold Cream doesn't have bronzer in it, because it is meant to be wiped off your face loaded with old makeup and dead skin cells. The distinction can be traced much further back in history. The ancient Romans had baths separate from their vomitoriums; and before them, in ancient Egypt, oil was kept in places of honor while water remained pretty much in the Nile. You might say, in fact, that cleaning and beautifying are like oil and water; they don't mix well, if at all.

Let's break down the items one would find in a standard bathroom by their cleaning or beautifying functions.

If you really think about it, your personal beautification process (it doesn't matter if you're a man or a woman) is very different from your body's cleaning and elimination systems. Why would you want to do all of that in the same room?

By suggesting that there is no distinction between cleaning and beautifying, the perfection-mongers at large have caused us to clutter up our bathrooms with unnecessary storage and unnatural behavior. Take the hair dryer, for instance. We all know that electricity and water are a bad pair, yet we think nothing of plugging in near the sink. Think of all the wrinkles you could have avoided if moisturizer were kept on your nightstand instead of in the faraway bathroom.

	CLEANING	BEAUTIFYING
Soap	Yes	—
Toothpaste	Yes	—
Hair dryer	—	Yes
Shampoo/conditioner	Yes	—
Hair spray/gel	—	Yes
Toothbrush	Yes	—
Curling iron	—	Yes
Makeup	—	Yes
Nail polish	—	Yes
Toilet paper	Yes	—
Towels	Yes	—
Face/body moisturizers	—	Yes
Emery board	—	Yes

Beautifying products such as makeup and perfume don't belong in the bathroom. Here they are placed on an old factory shoe rack in the bedroom.

reverse migration: into the lair

THE BEAUTY STATION

Remove all of your beauty items, and place them in a designated, well-lit place in your bedroom. It's really a throwback to the dressing table of old, where one would sit before a mirror to beautify oneself. If you have a small and overloaded bathroom now, you'll appreciate just how spacious it becomes. Additionally, if you find that you have too much beauty stuff, take the opportunity to throw out what you don't use, and learn to buy what you use instead of buying what magazines tell you the hottest new products are.

If, on the other hand, you have a large, redone bathroom with cabinets that were meant to store beauty products, I would still encourage you to establish a beauty station in your bedroom. Too much perfect storage begets hidden clutter; you probably can't deny that those shelves and drawers only encourage you to buy unnecessarily in bulk.

PRIVATE MEDICINE

Prescription pills are a private thing; you shouldn't place them in a bathroom if it is a public one. While you can trust your friends (well, who doesn't love a delicious bit of gossip?), children and strangers who may harbor untoward proclivities may come too close to your prescriptions. Even over-the-counter drugs should be discreetly stored. Nobody needs to know you use toe-fungus medication.

Place your prescription drugs in a reliquary in your bedroom or in a less obvious spot near your drinking water.

SIMPLIFYING TOILETRIES

When you begin to understand that the bathroom functions solely to cleanse the body, you easily realize how few toiletries you actually need. They can all be stored efficiently in the most rudimentary bathroom setup; in fact, since most of these items are used evenly either at the sink or in the shower, you don't even need a cabinet.

THE HEAD

Toothbrush
Toothpaste
Mouthwash
Dental floss
Facial cleanser
Razor
Shaving cream
Shampoo
Conditioner
Cotton swabs

ARMS AND HANDS

Hand soap
Nail brush
Fingernail clipper

LEGS AND FEET

Foot file or pumice stone
Toenail clipper

BACK AND TORSO

Body soap
Body brush

To ensure that you don't outgrow your bathroom, simply resist buying more than one of each toiletry at a time. If you have clutter, you can't have *gai*. Style really is an efficient system of use and replacement. It ain't inventory.

LEFT: In lieu of a vanity, an art box holds toiletries. Its small size keeps unnecessary junk in check.
OPPOSITE: An aesthetically pleasing bathroom is not all space and storage. Antiques and art give more style to it than tile and glass ever can.

SINKS AND MIRRORS

As much as decorators love to talk about the beauty of function, it is exactly what they seek to cover. What's wrong with plumbing? Is a water line so visually horrific that it must be housed in a cabinet? What does this cover-up say about the evanescence of decor itself?

If you've got a vanity, don't rip it out just because I'm railing against them. Give the money instead to a relative or friend in need. Keep the vanity, and clean it out so that the access to the water lines and drain is as uncluttered as possible.

If you need to replace your vanity, do so with a simple pedestal or wall-mounted sink. Dare to leave the plumbing exposed, and challenge your plumber to be artful with materials and execution. Place your toothbrush, toothpaste, and razor in your medicine cabinet, if you've got one. Otherwise, leave them plainly exposed, where they will look perfectly fine and stylish if you clean up as you should.

OPPOSITE: This tiny hand sink with bare plumbing is utilitarian and pleasing. The fixture was meant for a standard-size sink, but it works great here visually, extending the curve of the water pipes.

SIMPLE SHOWERS

A simple glass door on a shower or a basic old-school tub is a good feature that saves the aggravation of replacing shower curtains. That said, a basic clear heavy plastic shower curtain hung with standard metal or plastic rings is equally efficient. While all-white tile and walls certainly communicate sterility and cleanliness, a regular cleaning is the real thing. Whatever the color of your tile or walls, clear glass and plastic are both clean-looking and lazy-proof, meaning they actually have to be clean to look clean.

EVERYDAY CLEANUP

Think about it. We clean up the kitchen immediately after we eat, yet we don't bother to do the same in the bathroom. Food is less, well, gross than the dead skin cells and body wastes we eliminate, though we appropriate more attention and vigor in disinfecting our cooking surfaces than our toilets. We clean the bath far less than we use it, which not only lacks *gai,* it's strange.

A small bottle of multiuse, antibacterial spray cleanser with bleach is a prudent product to keep in the bathroom. Put it on the floor behind the toilet-bowl tank (right next to the bowl brush). Make it a family habit to spray the toilet rim and seat, wiping up with toilet tissue, which you can easily flush. After using the sink, spray and wipe with toilet tissue as well. If a bit of toothpaste gets on the mirror, spray and wipe. And to keep mold to a minimum, spray the same bottle in the shower regularly.

DESIGN CHECK: THE AGGRAVATION COST OF TILE

We see it all the time: bathroom makeovers that favor tile over wood floors, linoleum counters, and fiberglass showers. Tile has an aesthetic that can understandably be more pleasing: it looks rich; it's heavy and socially prestigious. But it's a nightmare to clean and repair. Grout fails, and water, mold, and slime easily grow under it. You could spend far less money for a very good-looking shower made of fiberglass and glass with far fewer time bombs.

Decorating divas hate to suggest wood in bathrooms, ignoring that wood is exactly what the *Niña,* the *Pinta,* and the *Santa María* were made of when Christopher Columbus sailed the seas. We trust wood in the form of siding to keep the elements out of our houses yet are loath to use it on the floor or walls of our bathrooms.

If you are considering redoing your bathroom, remember this: you can save a lot of money and aggravation by avoiding tile altogether.

TOWELS AND WASHCLOTHS

We dry off more ways than with just a towel. We can't immediately start pulling on our clothes after a towel-dry, because they'd stick to us, so we instinctively allow ourselves a few moments to air-dry after we towel off. Now, think for a moment about what would happen if we took a few moments in the shower before we reached for the towel — simply allowing the water on our skin to run off a little bit first. We'd need less towel, wouldn't we?

I have known people to spend a boatload of money on garishly large bathrooms inspired by the perception that they have no space for towels. Fifteen thousand unnecessary dollars later, they're just as damp after the towel-dry. The standards of bathroom perfection are not aligned with our real lives and schedules, which by and large are money-tight and time-short. Thirty measly seconds of thoughtful pause can literally reduce not only the size of your dream bathroom but the number of towels itself.

I often follow this practice and dry off with a hand towel. The important lesson is that linen style isn't reduced to a line of towels and sheets or rules of decor. It is articulated by behavior.

Washcloths are cool to keep in abundance, although compared with sponges, loofahs, exfoliating gloves, and so on, they don't perform as well. They're an excellent alternative to hand towels for one-time use since they are so easy to wash.

common sense updated: bath linen rethought

FOUR-STAR FANCY:

Washcloth

Because they're inexpensive and easy to wash, replace standard hand towels with a clean stack of easy-wash, one-time-use washcloths.

MINIMALIST GERMOPHOBE:

Hand towel

If you allow yourself to drip for a few moments in the shower, a hand towel easily dries off the rest of your body. If you're a clean freak, a stack of them replaces your germ-prone cotton bath mats.

TREAT FOR REGULAR FOLKS: Bath sheet

Go for the gusto. Ditch the bathrobe and standard-size towel, and wrap yourself in a bath sheet.

BATHROOM MATS

Bathroom mats, those you step on out of the shower, should probably be changed more often than we are prone to do. Stock up on three to five reversible, all-cotton (no rubber backing) ones that are easy to wash. If you're a germophobe, why not use hand towels as an easy-wash alternative?

Now, if you're using a cotton rug in a decorative sense, such as in front of a sink, use a decorative rug, for Pete's sake. A small wool Oriental is good-looking, and it repels water better than a cotton rug, anyway.

TOILET PAPER AND TISSUES

Don't keep a designer basket of TP on the floor; that's germy. Buy it in single rolls, keeping one on the roll and a backup roll on the tank. I find that tissues and TP in the bathroom are redundant. In privacy, who cares if you blow your nose on a bit of the roll, right?

Style isn't redundant. It's smart, efficient, and economical.

To me, a simple piece of string is infinitely more pleasing than a wall-mounted toilet-paper dispenser.

PART IV

HOW TO FUSS

closets

We still migrate, you know. As much as we may fancy ourselves the less savage cultivators, we hunt and gather with as much vigor as the original humanoid ancestor who achieved nothing too much more extraordinary than mere squirreling — as in *squirrel*. Our contemporary migrations have less to do with nutrition or the equinox than they do with unnecessary accumulation. Our behavioral mapping is navigated by excess rather than necessity, the major difference being that the location of our loot remains static.

There's that disconnection again. Squirrels adjust where and how they squirrel, according to where, how, and what they hunt and gather. We simply hunt and gather without much regard to the dynamics of how and where we store. We just figure that if we have big closets, all is right with the world, that we're livin' in high style if we have plenty of storage, heat, and/or air-conditioning.

By the way, few things are more wasteful — and quite frankly stupid — than the notion of a dream closet, and I personally have never met anyone with one whose wardrobe warranted the curatorial level of storage that said dream closet promised. Ample storage does not add to your personal style; in fact, the more space you have to store junk, the more prone you are to being a fashion victim.

In the earlier chapters, you learned that one of the ways toward *gai* is to shake storage up a little bit. And now we're about to bust some perfect storage notions with a little three-step system I call Closet Rescue.

CLOSET RESCUE
STEP 1.

EMPTY the linen closet

BUNDLE YOUR SHEETS Separate your sheets into bundled sets, dividing them, along with blankets and duvets, according to their respective beds.

DIVIDE YOUR BATH LINEN Also divide your bath towels and washcloths equally among the beds (or people in your home). Note: Keep the sheet and towel bundles to the side until the end of step 2.

DEAL WITH WHAT'S LEFT If you've got old quilts, take them out and use them as bed skirts, or throw them onto a chair or sofa in place of impersonal, newer throws. Donate the latter to your local charity shop.

PREPARE THE CLOSET Clean the now-empty linen closet in preparation for step 2.

CLOSET RESCUE
STEP 2.

RETHINK your regular closet

ONE-YEAR TEST Look at everything in your closet for things you haven't worn in one year. Separate them, and give them to your local charity shop. Don't worry about saving them for when you're skinny again or they come back in style.

DIVIDE BY SEASON Organize your remaining clothes, shoes, and accessories by season, removing the off-season clothes from their hangers and folding them as if you worked at the Gap. Fold off-season jackets and suits, too; even if you'd left them hanging, they'd still need a dry cleaning before you wore them again, because of creases caused by hanging too long.

OLD LINEN CLOSET BECOMES OFF-SEASON CLOSET Store your off-season wardrobe in your old linen closet until you need it again.

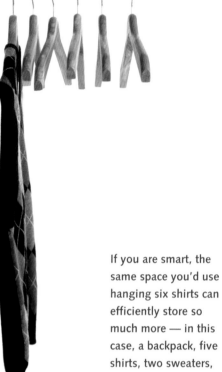

If you are smart, the same space you'd use hanging six shirts can efficiently store so much more — in this case, a backpack, five shirts, two sweaters, a pair of shoes, and a pair of boots.

REGULAR CLOSET BECOMES MULTIPURPOSE Because your regular closet is now less full, you may shelve your bed linens and towels next to your jeans and sweaters. Continue to fold your clothes Gap-style throughout the season; doing so conserves space and is kinder to your clothes.

MIGRATE SEASONALLY As the seasons change, switch the wardrobes between your bedroom closet and your off-season closet.

HANGING VERSUS FOLDING There are so many fantastic advantages to folding your shirts and slacks over hanging them, the least of which is saving space. Consider that in the space occupied by ten dress shirts on individual hangers, you can easily store twenty folded shirts, sheets, towels, six pairs of shoes, and a handbag or two.

If you iron your shirts, simply fold them, or if you have them laundered, ask your dry cleaner to return them to you boxed, which does not cost extra. If you travel often, packing a suitcase becomes much easier.

CLOSET RESCUE
STEP 3.

MAINTAIN your item count

BUY TO REPLACE To prevent buildup of clothes and linens that you don't use, simply buy to replace. Every time you buy one pair of jeans, donate an old pair, and so on. Purchase new linens and towels the same way.

BUY LESS BUT BETTER If you start buying less but better quality, it is less wasteful of resources such as the labor, material, and transport that went into making your clothing. It also saves you time and space. Most of all, it's so *gai*.

BE YOUR OWN STYLIST You don't always have to buy new clothes to get new outfits. Wardrobe stylists make a ton of money customizing regular clothes for their celebrity clients, and usually it's just done with a pair of scissors and some artful ripping. Regular folks like us can turn jeans or khakis into cool cutoffs of any length for the summer, and women can take slacks to the dry cleaner to have them hemmed knee- or capri-length for an entirely different look.

TURNING PANTS INTO SHORTS WITH A RAW EDGE

1. **CUT** Cut your jeans or khakis to desired length, leaving a ½-inch allowance for edge.

2. **DEWEAVE** Pull horizontally woven threads out. Use the point of a pin to separate the threads, if you need to.

3. **TRIM** Trim the pulled threads. If you like, you can run a piece of sandpaper along the edge to give your new shorts an appealing worn feel.

the way to cull

You own basically two categories of clothes: (1) those you wash and wear and (2) those you worship. It's easy enough to determine the clothes you wash and wear by giving yourself a simple test.

WASH-AND-WEAR TEST

For ten days, chart exactly the clothes you wear that go from your body to the laundry or dry cleaner and back onto your body. This will reveal a lot about how few of the clothes you own you actually wear. Every now and then I'll catch myself looking into my closet at perfectly good T-shirts but wanting to wear the one that's in the laundry. I'll do this over and over again for several months until one day I accept that I'm neither washing nor wearing several things. Then out they go to the charity shop.

If you conduct this test seasonally during a year, you'll know exactly how much clothing you actually need and want; for example, five T-shirts, three pairs of jeans, and so on. When you get to that place, you can walk into stores

It's disgustingly vulgar to amass more shoes than you can wear in two weeks.

knowing that if you want a new T-shirt, the most you really want is five.

Clothes you worship, however, are a beast of another species that can't be culled quite so easily because they are bound to you emotionally. Administer the SLAVE test to them, and watch what happens. As the SLAVE test reveals, original, custom-made things have *gai;* but there is no rational reason to worship something you bought off the rack that was made in a factory.

VULGARITY TRAP: SHOES AND BAGS

I, like my father before me, am a boot man. I don't care for loafers, or wingtips, or classic Oxfords. I suppose I don't even care about the popular notion of comfort. I love a hard leather sole and a sturdy three-inch Cuban heel, James Brown–style. Living in Maine, which is the land of fleece and comfort, I will admit that I stick out. People have actually asked me why I'd want to wear such an unversatile shoe. I tell them, if, God forbid, I were hit by a bus, I'd want the person who witnessed my last breath to say, "Nice boots."

In fact, I don't care to own more than two pairs of boots at a time. I am content to have one really good pair and retire it when it moves past a pleasing state of worn. Boots, alternating pairs of running shoes, an old pair of running shoes for chores such as painting, winter boots, and two-dollar flip-flops in the summer. That's it for me.

I realize that I have a rather severe shoe inventory and that most people need a few more pairs than I do. Still, it is disgustingly vulgar to amass more shoes than you can wear in two weeks. That's my cutoff, sorry. Sarah Jessica Parker notwithstanding, there are better things to spend your money on. I'm not saying not to live well or not to spend your hard-earned cash — absolutely, you should indulge yourself. But you can eat better cuts of meat, you can go on vacation, you can certainly give it away. You can just save it. A you-can't-have-too-many-shoes fetish fueled by the media has amounted to nothing more than advanced human squirreling. Ask yourself, do you want to have style, or do you want to be a rodent?

The same thing goes for bags. One bag per season and one evening bag. That's five, tops.

seasonal gear and the unexpected closette

One of the brilliant things about imperfection is that it is rich ground for genius. Making do with what you've got has yielded really singular and stylish storage ideas, my favorite example being the "floating jar of nails." You know it, I'm sure. One day long ago, someone figured out that if old jar lids were nailed onto the underside of a garage shelf, you could put things in the jar part, screw it into the nailed lid, and voilà! Clean, genius organization that passes the SLAVE test with flying colors.

A closette is a storage opportunity that already exists. It isn't a cutesy clear plastic number you fill with junk. It is a found storage solution that relieves your closets; it doesn't cost extra, and you've already got it.

A SUMMER CLOSETTE: COOLER OR ICE CHEST

If you've got one of these and break it out during the summer for picnics and barbecues, in the fall put it away filled with:

- BEACHWEAR, BATHING SUITS
- BEACH TOWELS
- BEACH BAGS
- FLIP-FLOPS
- SANDALS
- SUMMER HATS

In the off-season, these items won't crap up your closets. Be sure that your cooler is clean and dry before you use it as a closette.

A WINTER CLOSETTE: THE HUGE HOLIDAY SUITCASE

- WINTER COATS
- SWEATERS
- WINTER ACTIVEWEAR
- BOOTS
- SCARVES, CAPS, GLOVES
- COLD-WEATHER BED LINENS

Most of our trips may involve only an overnight bag, but if we live far enough away from our hometown, we usually reserve a huge piece of luggage for holiday plane travel. It's a necessity for lugging gifts and/or packing heavier and thicker winter clothes. Big suitcases are a great storage opportunity for cold-weather outerwear and bed linens.

A SEASONAL CLOSETTE: BAGS AND PURSES

Why would you want to put a purse away for the season empty? Isn't a little bit of filling in its cavity recommended to keep its shape anyway? Seasonal accessories such as neck scarves, fashion or costume jewelry, sunglasses, and certain types of hosiery can easily fit into that season's bag and be tucked neatly out of the way until you need them again.

- SILK SCARVES
- SEASONAL JEWELRY
- WALLET
- SUNGLASSES

other closette opportunities

careful that it doesn't become a junk trunk — keep it clean and organized as though it were a closet. Migrate the contents seasonally, storing beach towels and blankets in the summer and an extra sweater or wool socks in the winter.

HANGER If you have lots of belts, why not pull their buckles over a hanger hook and organize them with the slacks or skirts you like? Ditto if you're a scarf person; match them with your blouses. There's a great advantage to this: you get to plan your outfits in advance.

OFFICE If you have "work shoes," leave them there. If you're in the health-care field, I beg you to keep your scrubs at work. There are few things more alarmingly disgusting to me than when I see a health-care worker at the supermarket after work touching fruits, vegetables, and bread. What microscopic mayhem is lurking? Keep it at work, where it belongs.

GYM LOCKER If you belong to a gym, you can relieve your home closet by storing your clean gym clothes and shoes in your locker. Simply bring your sweaty clothes home and return them to the locker when they have been laundered. If your locker is large enough, you can also store your gym towels.

CAR TRUNK If you're an outdoors lover, you can store things such as hiking boots, tennis shoes, Windbreakers, and golf shoes in your trunk. Be

GEAR BAGS Bike clothing doesn't have to add to the density of your off-season closet during the winter. Instead, it can stay in your backpack. Similarly, if you reserve a fine attaché case for your most important business meetings, you can put your best business shirt and tie right in it. And if you have a wrinkle-free dress or two that you keep just for traveling, relieve your closet by keeping them in a piece of luggage.

NIGHTSTANDS

Let's face it, our nightstands are never too large — a glass of water, a good book, some moisturizer, maybe a snack, and before we know it, it's crowded. Standard nightstands, by design, are horribly inefficient pieces of furniture. But if you expand your idea of what it ought to be, you can create a good closette opportunity quite easily.

I bought an old flour barrel in London (what was I thinking?), shipped the damn thing back, and wondered what to do with it. I put it through the SLAVE test and realized that it was an important symbol of how dumb I used to be about style, so I decided to make it adaptable. Today I use it as my nightstand, into which goes off-season duvets and blankets.

DRESSERS

A bit of obvious wisdom: if your dressers are too full, you're junked up — ain't no other answer. Beware of drawer "organizers." They're usually strips of plastic that divide a drawer into sections for socks, underwear, ties, and so on. Though not so obvious, these are junk traps nonetheless.

OPPOSITE: I bought this flour bin while on a trip to England in 1996. It is both my nightstand and my linen closet.

Why? Convenience. It's not convenient to roll your underwear so it looks like a *bento* box of Japanese lunch. That's just too much work. It is far easier to administer the wash-and-wear test to the items in your drawer and cull the unused items. Life is good if you can throw socks into a drawer that isn't overcrowded and doesn't jam when you try to close it.

UNDERBED STORAGE

If, and only if, you have a studio apartment or a bedroom closet that doesn't have the capacity to store clothes that pass the wash-and-wear test, then store your things under the bed. Otherwise, all you're going to do is stick unnecessary stuff into a plastic underbed storage coffin and give yourself a poor excuse to clean out hidden dirt on a regular basis.

Plus, how can you deny the little ones in your life (be they children or pets) an essential spot for hide-and-seek?

basements, ETC.

About ten years ago, I decided I wanted some climbing roses. I suppose I'd always been the kind of guy who believed way too much in miracles and knew nothing about garden pests. I hadn't even known of the Japanese beetle until the spring of 1996, when my New Dawn climbers unfurled their energetic leaves, from which burst the most breathtaking pink roses I'd ever seen that weren't silk. Within twelve hours of their freshman performance, every bloom was covered with the beetles. In those days I didn't know about the deadly insecticide malathion, so all I could do was watch helplessly as the sun set on my New Dawn — and buy a too-late boatload of malathion.

At the advice of the rose grower (who was in Texas), I cut the roses to the ground and sprayed my yard with hundreds of dollars' worth of organic beneficial nematodes. The grower also suggested that I do all I could to prevent moisture from collecting on the roots and leaves, which translated into a system of trellises I hadn't really planned on. "Absolutely!" I told the rose guy. "I can do that."

So off I went shopping for trellises, but as you know, I have this singularity thing. I couldn't really stomach most of what I found, and the trellises that did attract me were so ridiculously expensive that, well, every man has his limits. Then one day while watching PBS, I got an idea from Norm Abram on *The New Yankee Workshop*. It looked easy, it was cedar, and who cared that I couldn't recognize a miter if it blew my house away. **Still, like a fool, I turned my basement into a veritable wood shop.** Circular saw, workbench, miter box, and all. For a trellis.

What I haven't yet said is that the basement was already filled with a NordicTrack we never used, old furniture from Jen's parents that I hadn't yet had the style to incorporate, and old boxes of books and junk. In short, the basement was already full. But hey, there's always space for a money-saving project around the house, right? Wrong.

the role of basements and attics

Dogs lick themselves because they can, and our basements and attics become junk-filled because we can make them that way. The difference between dogs and us, though, is that dogs are really keeping things clean, while we're just wasting time and resources.

If most of us were in the state of *gai,* or had true style, there would be no such thing as Grandmother's china in a box in the attic or Mom's old table sitting dusty in the basement. We would surround ourselves with these items instead of chasing style by replacing emotion and legacy with something from a popular decor store.

At one point in history, the basement made

excellent sense. In the days before refrigeration, the cellar was an efficient way to store food throughout the cold months and, in some cases, livestock whose body heat would help keep the inhabitants of the floors above warm. In the grandest homes throughout the world, basements still bustle with servants who prepare meals and laundry. From a utilitarian standpoint, the basement worked best when it had everything to do with the life upstairs. Laundry and rec rooms notwithstanding, when basements today are used for storage, they tend to be one gigantic junk drawer, a sad reliquary of the connection to our past that has stopped or been abandoned altogether.

In the same way, attics in contemporary life have become indoor dumps for things we don't use anymore. The taste for cathedral ceilings and improved insulation materials have all but eliminated attics in new construction, and it is common to turn them into bedrooms or everyday living space in older homes. But if an unconverted attic exists, chances are it's got junk. And a lot of it.

what you should not store

THINGS YOU'LL NEVER USE

Because attics and basements are larger than most closets, whatever stuff we park there tends to stay and go into what I call storage purgatory. We can neither commit them to the heaven of everyday use or the hell of garbage — or so we think. By filling our attics and basements with junk, we're really making our own lives hell. Whenever I'm in my basement, I ask myself, "When I die, are my friends and family who come and clean out my house going to look at all my stuff and say, 'What is all this crap?'" The thought that they wouldn't recognize it is terrifying.

It is recognition that breaks the purgatorial state. You must recognize that either (1) the stuff is junk and should be thrown out, or (2) you've got a connection to it and should incorporate it into your everyday life in your everyday rooms.

I did actually make the rose trellis and was quite happy with it. But I never used my saw and miter box again and after a few years realized that they were in purgatory. I recognized that I would never be that handy again. I didn't want to be! And so they became expensive junk. I hope the person I gave them to continues to find them useful.

THINGS YOU'LL NEVER FIX

You should only bring a fixer-upper chair or table, or whatever, home if (1) you can fix it within ten days, and (2) you can fix it without having to buy one tool, special gadget, or paint. Otherwise, ten days will turn into ten weeks, then ten years.

Steer clear of projects you dream you'll have time for at some vague point in the future. Basements are dirty enough without having to hoard this clutter.

THINGS YOU PLAN ON DONATING

What are you waiting for? Give it away, already. I knew someone who, for years, held on to books she intended to donate to her library. By the time she got around to making her gift, the library wasn't interested. You aren't being generous while you're sitting on the loot. You're just procrastinating.

THINGS FOR FAMILY AND FRIENDS

If family members or friends own something that doesn't fit in their house, then it's not adaptable to their life as it is today and is therefore not stylish anyway. Don't let their nonsense turn into your storage purgatory. Just say hell no.

THINGS FOR ENTERTAINING

If you've got a basement or attic that contains special tables, tablecloths, dishes, and centerpieces that you keep to use for when you entertain at home, I don't want to come to your house. Hospitality isn't putting on a show, it's being intimate with people in your natural habitat.

household heirlooms

As I've said, you ought to live with your heirlooms, not delegate them to a dark, dusty area or throw them away. They should be kept in the family even if your family members are grossed out by the idea.

HOW, THEN, DO YOU PASS THINGS ON?

1. Find another relative who'll take it. If your misguided sister won't use it, find a cousin and tell him or her how important it is that he or she help carry on the family history.

2. Start teaching the young members of the family how cool it is to own something that's been part of the group for years. They all grow up too fast, and before you know it, you can pass it on.

3. Find out what was important to the relative who passed away. Did he or she like birds? Sell it, and make a donation to the Audubon Society in your relative's name. Maybe the relative had a best friend who might appreciate its significance too.

WHAT'S OKAY TO STORE

1. **HOLIDAY DECORATIONS:** artificial Christmas trees, wreaths and garlands, ornaments, novelties, holiday wrapping paper, cards, etc.

3. **RECREATIONAL EQUIPMENT:** ice chests, camping equipment, tents, sleeping bags, etc.

2. **SPORTS EQUIPMENT:** bikes, helmets, kayaks, skis, racquets, balls, nets, golf clubs, etc.

everyday heirlooms

Make any hand-me-down tablecloth fit by using knots at the corners to shorten it.

Grandma's champagne glasses are cooler than new flutes.

Clean up an old skillet instead of getting a trendy new one.

A cracked bowl becomes a one-of-a-kind vessel for a potted plant.

Bring an old pair of scissors to the knife shop and have them sharpened.

Mom's old doll packs much more decorative impact than anything new.

DIY DISORDER: *The condition of pursuing specialized tools for one-time do-it-yourself projects. This is a very bad thing to have.*

When all else fails, put the heirloom in a clean box that you'll seal. Inside, leave a note about its provenance, why it was important for you to keep, and that you hope someone else finds it and welcomes it into his or her family.

everyday tools and supplies

One day I brought a lamp that needed a new switch into my local hardware store. It was admittedly a small problem, but I'm not handy that way. I'm not ashamed to admit it, even though all the decorating divas on TV make it look so easy. The fix may very well have involved an exceedingly elementary maneuver, but I'd rather go for a walk than pretend I'm mildly interested in being in the lamp-repair business. Anyway, my intention was to have the service desk fix it for me.

The service guy told me they could do it, that it would take a week, and why on earth didn't I just fix it myself? I replied, in part, "I don't even think I have all the tools to fix it." (The other part of my answer I transported telepathically and went something like, "Listen, yo, you're the darn hardware man.") "Well, that's why I have all my own tools, so

that if something happens, I won't need to borrow anyone else's," the service guy said.

His response confirmed a sneaking suspicion I'd had for a while: that we're a country with too many damn tools. God forbid we have to borrow a special tool from someone else. Shame on us that we don't have one. Bad domestic god! Terrible domestic goddess! Whatever.

Forget that kind of thinking. Unless you are a full-time electrician and plumber and carpenter and tile layer and mason, you really need only a few tools. If your basement or attic or garage is cluttered, you probably have do-it-yourself disorder.

There isn't any reason for two neighbors, or siblings who live close to each other, to own their own chainsaws, air compressors, or jackhammers. If you are afraid of borrowing from the neighbor for fear of embarrassment, your social skills need more work than whatever your project is.

Now, if someone came to you to borrow a tool and you refused because you've got a history of loaning things that don't come back, that's your own problem. Have some *gai,* and ask for it back — clearly you don't care for it enough that you would pursue it after its use. So if that was your reason for turning a request down, shame on you. You could have really made a difference in how that person's day went.

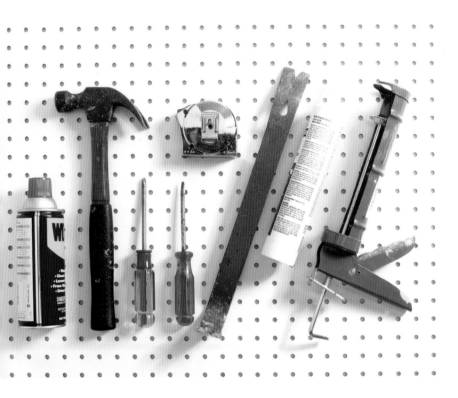

MAINTAINERS: POUND, SCREW, OR ATTACH

Hammers, screwdrivers, nails, nuts, bolts, and screws for everyday use. If you take your screwdrivers around the house and take a good look at your cabinets, appliances, and furniture you can easily determine what screws you need on hand. A tube of latex caulk and a caulk gun is handy for people in older homes but not entirely necessary in newer ones or apartments.

CUTTERS AND TWISTERS

Basic wood and pipe saw, wire cutters, utility knife, vise grips, and wrenches. Be sure that your gripping tools are clean and operable. Few things are more frustrating than trying to use a rusted wrench.

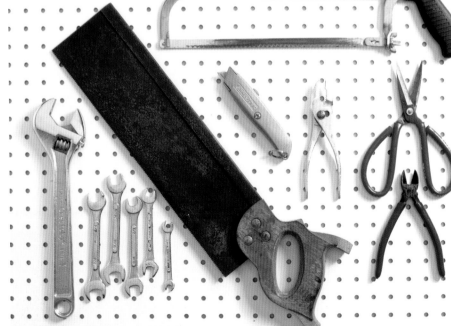

BEAUTIFIERS: COLOR, POLISH, OR BUFF

Paintbrushes, rollers, trays, painting supplies, sandpaper, and small sanders. A good tip for storing paint in cans is to put its clean lid on, tapping it so that it is tight and secure on the can. Then turn it upside down on a piece of newspaper for later use. This prevents a skin from forming at the surface.

ROPE, STRING, AND TAPE

A ball of hemp string goes a long way, as does a roll of duct tape, clothesline, rope, and a bit of craft wire.

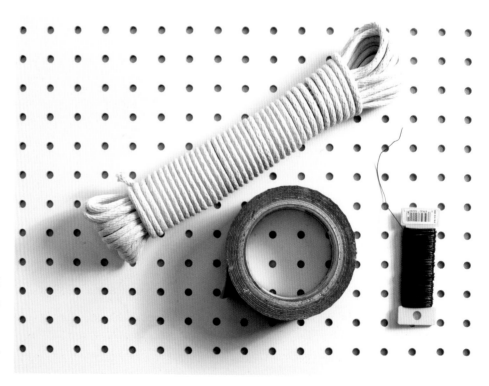

storing gardening supplies

Back in my giant-garden days, I had a perfectly appointed garden shed that matched the house. Today I live in the middle of an old city, and my gardening is limited to along the driveway and in a small patch of lawn that abuts a cobbled sidewalk. So I have to store gardening supplies in my very old, haunted basement. I've learned that you absolutely do not need the perfect potting shed to be an organized gardener. All you need is a little bit of cleaning sense.

POTS

Empty pots of soil onto a pile in a discreet corner of your garden (such as under a tree or bush).

Instead of washing them in a sink, scrub them in your driveway with the same gusto you'd summon for washing your car. Dry them upside down, and stack them inside each other for storing.

FERTILIZERS AND INSECTICIDES

Use less. I use only one kind of fertilizer: fish emulsion. In fact, my entire garden is based on how much fertilizing I wanted to deal with, which is very little.

Buy bottles of insecticides ready to apply, meaning they have spray attachments. Avoid bulk and refill sizes — you don't want to touch that stuff anyway.

CUTTERS AND SHOVELS

Brush clean and wipe with a clean cloth. Spray on a bit of WD-40 to keep them oiled and working well.

A MOMENT OF *GAI*

I learned a few years ago that sometimes one ritual can clarify an entire process and philosophy. For example, to my in-laws, cooking a turkey meant that they were going to address and discuss a problem. At first I found it comical, but over the years I understood that the turkey was a kind of "bell" that everyone recognized as a call for action or change.

For me, a similar "bell" is washing my garden hose. When it becomes obvious that it needs to come off its spigot or else a freeze might threaten plumbing havoc, I bring it to the middle of my driveway, give it a soapy wash, and dry it completely. I think about how thankful I am for the season that's just past and how lucky I am to be alive. Throughout the winter, the clean hose reminds me not to junk up the basement; and in the spring, the cycle of *gai* begins anew.

46
elm street

Hours:

7:00 a.m.–6:30 p.m.

8:00 a.m.–90 p.m.

DRY

SAME

SHI

AL

WED

SUED

CHAPTER THIRTEEN

STYLE FROM THE *'hood*

The notions of domestic perfection have gotten us all to behave like inefficient consumers. Instead of going out to spend our hard-earned money on well-deserved products, we're spending it on supplies to make them. It's no secret that it is difficult to schedule quality time with our families and friends, yet it is curious that the pressure to emulate the so-called good life that the domestic divas incessantly hawk eliminates much of that time we have left so that we can . . . uh . . . make a greeting card. Or a headboard.

Consumers are also experiencing a customer-service crisis. It is nearly impossible to get live assistance on a customer-service line anymore. If that do-it-yourself headboard has a problem with the silk material you stapled to it, do you really think the fabric store is going to stand by it? Of course not. You are your own vice president of customer satisfaction.

Step away from the glue gun, yo. It's a very dangerous weapon. Buy the dang greeting card. Have the headboard delivered.

Since I took that broken lamp to my local hardware store to have its switch fixed, I've completely embraced my abject inability for certain kinds of DIY. I've brought in picture frames that needed sprucing up and a hose that required a new female end. Once I dropped off a dog lead that needed to be shortened so our energetic puppy, Frances Margaret, could safely enjoy what sun she could in our city driveway. In order for me to have completed that job, I would have had to purchase a table-mounted vise and a heavy-duty cable snipper, the kind that the *Ocean's Eleven* crew use to make a living. Instead, I hopped into the car, drove down to the hardware store, and smiled at my new friends at the service desk. If I wait, I wait. The five bucks it costs to get it done by pros is nothing compared with the quality of the work and the savings on aggravation.

See? True style requires value, and the two ways to gauge value are money cost and aggravation cost. My hardware store service desk isn't the home wood shop certain magazines say I should have. It's better — it's got *gai*.

building your fuss network

Fuss network: **a value-based system that identifies others who can DIB (do it better).**

We are naturally drawn to efficiency. Our kids and bosses always ask us, "Say, if you can do that, would you mind doing this?" Chances are, if we can, we will. It doesn't hurt to ask service professionals if they are willing to expand upon their traditional menu of services.

Your personal fuss network will depend on the merchants and service businesses in your community. Since it doesn't exist yet, don't freak out when individuals you approach answer no. After all, they're not advertising that they'll do everything; but they might oblige if you deserve it, and you'll deserve it if you invest in a personal, cordial relationship first. In other words, date before you marry.

A fuss network is very cool. If you get one going, you can easily:

- SAVE MONEY AND AGGRAVATION
- SAVE TIME
- GET THINGS DONE BETTER
- SAVE SPACE
- IMPROVE YOUR SOCIAL SKILLS
- FOCUS ON THE MORE IMPORTANT THINGS

STEP 1.
IDENTIFY YOUR FUSS LANDSCAPE

List the merchants you regularly do business with, and try to imagine what else they could do for you. At the same time, note some of the things that you'd like to fuss over.

Never assault a merchant with your list. Establish rapport first. Make them want to help you out. Scratch their back, you know what I'm saying?

TURN A SHIRT BOX INTO A GIFT BOX

STEP 1: Find a shirt-box lid.

STEP 2: Flatten and fold so that bottom and top edges of the short sides meet. Crease well.

STEP 3: Repeat on other side to create a new fold at the center.

STEP 4: Open and cut along new side creases.

STEP 5: Fold shut. You can do the same thing to the bottom of the shirt box.

FUSS CENTER DRY CLEANER

YOUR QUANDARY	THEIR ABILITIES	YOU AVOID
Moths in your sweaters	Mothproof bags	Cedar closet supplies
Red wine stain on your cotton couch	Industrial-strength stain remover; ask them for a little	A whole bottle of stain remover that might not work
Lost button on your duvet cover	Buttons for every kind of need	A trip to the button store, if you even have one
A sheet or two of acid-free tissue	They've got it — they use it like toilet paper	A whole pack of tissue, plus somewhere to store it
Quick gift box	An inventory of shirt boxes	Having to buy a pack of gift boxes
Your arm length	An in-house tailor or seamstress	A tailor's tape measure; ordering the wrong size shirt
Adhesive label that refuses to be removed	A major steam machine	Grief; a bottle of adhesive remover

FUSS CENTER THE COBBLER

YOUR QUANDARY	THEIR ABILITIES	YOU AVOID
Faded leather chair	Dyes of every color	The runaround; the wrong bottle of dye
Dog chewed its leash in two	Really strong sewing machine	A new dog leash
Laptop on glasstop desk worries you	Round rubber heel protectors	A whole pack of round felt things; anxiety
Small bit of Formica has come unglued	Adhesives strong enough to walk on	An epoxy you'll use only once
You wish you were a little taller	They make heels taller	Napoleon complex; unused shoes
Kid keeps losing his scarf	Grommets — have them put one on the scarf and link to coat	Lost scarves; sad kid

STEP 2. IDENTIFY A FUSS MAP

While the cobbler and the dry cleaner are solid examples of fuss centers, you may very well live in a town with considerably less city slickness. Not to worry — rather than identifying fuss centers, you can map your network according to your quandary, reaching out over several merchants.

FUSS CENTER YOUR TOWN, USA

YOUR QUANDARY	MERCHANT	NOTES
Dull knives, cutters, and scissors	Butcher shop	They routinely employ a knife-sharpening service
You want to make crème brûlée	Plumber	He's got a portable torch
Need music for a special occasion	Library	Why buy when you can borrow for free?
Making a big cake, need a plate	Pizzeria	They've got the cardboard rounds
Looking for cool ideas for showerheads	Hairdresser	They have access to really cool plumbing accessories
Need pails	Bakery	Many ingredients such as jelly come in pails they might want to get rid of
A little bit of potting soil	Greenhouse	They've got it in bulk; you don't need to buy a bag
Wrap a small gift	Florist	They've got a ton of ribbon and wrapping paper
No space to hold recyclables	Sidewalk	If you've got a deposit program in your state, someone'll pick it up
An exotic flavoring for a special dessert	Coffee shop	Ask if you can buy a shot of one of their flavored syrups

When your fuss network allows you to reach out to those who do it better, something quite miraculous happens — you live better …

the DIB advantage

Saving time, money, space, and aggravation is the obvious advantage of establishing a fuss network; interacting with your community is an even more important one; and the ultimate is time with those you love. When your fuss network allows you to reach out to those who do it better, something quite miraculous happens: you live better and prettier without the compulsive need for domestic-diva television porno.

Perfection-mongers never tell you how to be where you are. Rather, they tell you that you should introduce their foreign ideas into your natural habitat so you can feel at home. That's just crazy. For example, hosting a combination homemade/takeout Thai dinner is better with the DIB approach. Stick to what you know you can successfully pull off.

DIB ENTERTAINING: THAI DINNER FOR FOUR

OBJECTIVES
1. Do what you do best.
2. Have the Thai restaurant do what they do best.

MENU
Summer Rolls with Shrimp and Peanut Sauce
Fresh Cucumber Salad with Lime and Cilantro
Red Curry with Grilled Flank Steak
Brown Rice with Petite Peas
Ginger Ice Cream

YOU CAN:
1. Make the cucumber salad.
2. Grill the flank steak.
3. Make brown rice, and throw in some frozen peas.
4. Serve vanilla ice cream with chopped crystallized ginger.

THEY CAN:
1. Make the summer rolls — you just have to drop off your platter.
2. Make the curry sauce — drop off your pot.
3. Deliver.
You *can* cook Thai in your un-Thai kitchen.
You don't have to buy one ounce of curry, fish sauce, rice paper — none of it.

If you're not great at setting a table, don't worry. You can do a lot with TV trays. Here they are positioned to create an impromptu and stylish setting for four.

your
DIB

Okay, we've figured out how everyone can help you, so now you must ask how can you help them. What of yourself are you willing to volunteer to this network?

Giving back doesn't require involving yourself with a ".org," or any kind of grand public gesture. It can be as easy as surprising the plumber whose propane torch you're going to borrow with his own dish of crème brûlée. You can involve yourself with the dry-cleaning lady to the extent that you know what issues she's working through in her life. Something as easily said as "Is there anything I can do for you?" goes a long way. But we're afraid of that question. We're too worried about our weight and storage solutions.

It all boils down to honesty. Anybody can, and should, ask of people in their lives, "Can I do anything for you?" And if you hear their request and know you can't deliver, just say you can't. Tell them you can't fix their broken lamp switch or lend them money, that you, yourself, drop that stuff off at the hardware store and are strapped for cash. But if you can help, you should be grateful that you can.

In this book's introduction I mentioned that people want only one thing: a sense of belonging. It cannot be achieved or sustained without mutual consent and effort. It's more important to make people feel that they belong to you, that they can ask even though they might not receive.

What are you putting dibs on? Fuss over your own list, and start being part of your neighborhood's conveniences.

PART V
HOW TO TEND

CHAPTER FOURTEEN

VASES, FLOWERS, AND *such*

Let me say right off the bat that you should have only one vase for every table surface in your house, and even that's too many. If by the benevolence of others and the universe you came into enough flowers to fill every room under your roof, you'd still be limited by the number of tables you've got to display them. Few of us are that lucky; you can see why keeping an equal ratio of tables to vases might be unnecessary and excessive.

One only needs to take a quick glance at the shelves of the local Salvation Army thrift store or a neighborhood rummage sale to surmise the extent of our vase overload. They're everywhere! Like some under-the-radar American pastime. When we get an arrangement sent from a florist, we know we're not interested in the vase, yet we can't bring ourselves to throw it out with the dead flowers. Instead, we rinse it clean and stick it somewhere discreet but respectful. The years go by, and before you know it, it's the attack of the FTD vases.

Adding to this vessel constriction is designer pressure to have several types of vases for different stems and buds. Tall ones for gladiolus and twigs, teeny-tiny ones for sweet pea, low and square with pebbles for forced bulbs. And then there's the frogs (those sea urchin–like implements for keeping flowers in place), the special scissors, the floral tape, the clear rubber bands, the live-longer powder. The simplicity of enjoying a bouquet of blooms has gotten really complicated.

traditional vases:
how to spot a keeper

RULE 1. THE VASE MUST LOOK GOOD EMPTY

Take the expensive, big, tall hurricane glass number for gladiolus that I mentioned previously. When it's empty, who cares? It needs to be filled with something other than dust to be interesting. Inexpensive can be boring, too. For example, old mason jars are completely forgettable. It makes no sense to collect them (as people do) for a casual summer tablescape. Every fall, winter, and spring you're going to open a few jars of pickles and spaghetti sauce anyway — you're set in the jar-as-vase department. Go for singularity and interest.

Whether or not it's holding flowers, this vase is art.

RULE 2. THE VASE SHOULD ENRICH YOU, NOT THE FLORIST

Some vases require far too many flowers to realize their design intent, so many that they can break the bank. A keeper vase is one that looks great whether you fill it with a few well-chosen stems or a lush, generous bouquet.

This trendy square vase only looks good when it is filled with a lot of flowers. A single stem looks really bad in it.

RULE 4. **THE VASE MUST DO ITS BASIC JOB**

If the vase can't sit on a table or needs some special gadget to make it work, then it's not really a utilitarian vessel; it's an unnecessary production.

Where the heck are you going to store a fragile, thigh-high hurricane vase? What a headache.

If it requires a hook and a wall, it ain't a vase.

RULE 3. **THE VASE MUST BE EASY TO STORE**

Vases must be easily stored in your cupboards and cabinets, or they must be interesting enough to be left out and stand on their own.

RULE 5. **FLORA SHOULD FALL NATURALLY IN A VASE**

This stem of bells of Ireland is cradled gorgeously in this lovely old rosewood container.

found vases and the high-low

It may be that because I'm an underdog myself, I am drawn to the unlikely vase. Having grown up on a remote island at a time when there weren't too many "cultured" domestic accoutrements, I learned to make do and appreciate what westerners love to call irony. In my mind, there's nothing ironic about an unspeakably fragrant bunch of jungle-grown tuberoses placed in an empty, slightly rusted Folgers coffee can — especially when your house just blew away. Designers have recognized this beguiling alchemy of exquisite flowers and lowly vessels in French country design and have attempted (in my opinion feebly) to replicate it in mass-produced tinware.

I suppose now is as good a time as any to differentiate fashion and style. Here's what I think: fashion costs; style can't be bought.

The great news is that your very own singular floral style is easily articulated with your own version of the High-Low. There is no dogmatic decorating here, just a couple of easy guidelines.

1. Look around for anything that holds water, paying special attention to the fact that it has absolutely nothing to do with flowers or decorating. In fact, the more unfloral, the better. But don't think about it too much. Let your instinct guide you.

2. If necessary, clean the vessel so that it can be placed on a table.

3. Fill with lush flowers.

Hydrangea in hen-and-chick creamer.

I suppose now is as good a time as any to differentiate fashion and style. Here's what I think: fashion costs; style can't be bought.

A child's beach pail with *Osteospermum* 'Lemon Symphony' effectively brings the outdoors inside at a summer cocktail party.

Every now and then my mom sends me a care package from home. One of my favorite things is salty, spicy Spanish-style chorizos packed in lard. Oy. The foot-tall cans are so beautiful that I use them as vessels, here as a spring arrangement with a potted *Sutera cordata* 'Snowstorm.'

houseplants

Gardening is for wimps, houseplants are for warriors. That sums up my fascination with houseplants. Clearly, I am in a continuous state of awe, hope, and frustration with the concept (and reality) of plants indoors.

For starters, they're highly unnatural, and throughout this book I've been arguing that style — *gai* — is a natural state. There ain't nothin' God-given about no staghorn fern in my bedroom in Maine, yo. And I don't care what anyone says, all houseplants are deli-

what if they want to be weeds? After all, like the maligned dandelion, which can survive anywhere, houseplants thrive in the most unlikely situations — in high-rises, doctors' offices, and banks. Plus, they live on unnatural foods and photosynthesize under artificial light; and because American homes are disproportionately larger than the rest of the homes on earth, houseplants may not even have enough carbon dioxide to exist, let alone grow.

While there is certainly very good evidence,

Once you acknowledge that houseplants are wild at heart, you can live with them in the state of gai and enjoy a stylish coexistence.

cate. I have, with scheduled water and food, killed philodendrons; I have, despite monitoring systems and gourmet soil, dried out cacti. Yet I'm a reasonably intelligent person; I look left and right twice before thinking about crossing the street. So you can, at the very least, imagine how fastidious I am about putting plants in their most advantageous spot, never mind the care they have on many occasions so carelessly discarded.

But one day it hit me. What if houseplants just want to be plants, instead of the specimens we force them to be? More to the point,

both researched and anecdotal, that houseplants do, in fact, benefit from water, light, and food — adjusted for their particular type — I cling to the merits of my weed theory, though, I admit, it is only valid in the less controversial behavior we call decor. Essentially, once you acknowledge that houseplants are wild things at heart, then you can live with them in the state of *gai* and enjoy a stylish coexistence.

Following are some of the weediest beauties available. They are hearty, individual, and decor-agnostic.

GIVING FLOWERS AND PLANTS

Gai: Pay it forward. When you give flowers and plants, keep the junk out of your friends' lives, too.

1. If sending flowers, send cut flowers instead of arrangements.

2. If giving flowers, bring them either cut or arranged in a vase of your own that can be returned later. Don't give them a vase you want to get rid of — that's just passing on junk.

3. When sending flowers, ask the florist to precut the stems to approximate a finished home arrangement. Most cut flowers have purposefully long stems so that professionals can use them in tall and large bouquets. Simple home bouquets are much smaller and shorter.

4. Houseplants are a horrible gift as a form of congratulations or an expression of condolence. They are a responsibility the receiver might not have time or space for.

5. If someone admires your houseplant, offer to give a cutting if it can be propagated. Plants grow.

ABOUT FAKES

Actually, I adore a really good fake flower (not so much plants, because you can easily obtain several varieties that are very difficult to kill). I realize there are purists out there who pooh-pooh the notion, which is, quite frankly, a bit ignorant. Don't we idolize fake imagery in painting and sculpture?

I say, if you're going for it, go for it, and offer no apologies. Choose flowers that are big, bright, and downright gaudy. That word *gaudy* makes me think of Spanish architect Antoni Gaudí, a surrealist rascal who considered ce-

This extremely fake plate-size Gerbera daisy is juxtaposed with a watercolor by famed old-Hollywood photographer George Daniel.

ramic sunflowers in relief a perfectly acceptable exterior surface. He had *gai.*

Again, go for the High-Low mix. Just as you would cradle exquisite French tulips in a rusted Foster's pint tin, how about a fakey-fake rose or two in your most expensive vessel? You might surprise yourself.

RELIABLE HOUSEPLANTS

MANDEVILLA (*Dipladenia* or *Mandevilla sanderi*). Also known as Brazilian jasmine. This luscious vine with velvety pink flowers does well in a tub or hanging in a sunny window. You need to water evenly and watch diligently for pests. A really glorious houseplant.

HOYA (*Hoya carnosa compacta*). Also known as Hindu rope. This easy-to-grow gorgeous, waxy vine sprouts tumbles of star-shaped flowers. With over two hundred varieties, leaf shape, texture, and flowers differ greatly. The best part: they like being root-bound and aren't too picky about light.

PARLOR PALM (*Chamaedorea elegans*). A super-hardy, delicate-looking, and well-shaped palm, it actually sprouts little "coconuts." It grows slowly, some say to five feet, although mine has remained happily under two feet for many years.

AFRICAN VIOLET ('Rhapsodie Patricia'). This is a standard violet with frilled, dark pink flowers and heart-shaped, dark green leaves. It's always good to keep violets because they seem to love the plastic pots they come in, which can drive you crazy if you're prone to repot into something more "fabulous." This plant quietly and beautifully teaches you focus and patience.

PEPEROMIA CLUSIIFOLIA ('Rainbow'). A popular groundcover in warmer zones, it is also a terrific potted plant that's pleasantly not so green, thanks to its yellow and pink margins. A great one for people who forget to water, it likes to dry out between waterings and, if given the chance, will gladly trail and mound in a well-lit (not necessarily sunny) spot.

PHILODENDRON. What can I say about these reliable gems? If you don't like them to trail, cut them back and stick the cuttings back into the pot to create a fuller effect. They're a communicative plant: if you water them too much, their leaves turn yellow; too little, they turn brown and fall off. A great legacy plant. I love the idea that plants get passed through generations.

TROPICAL BEGONIA ('Rhinestone Jeans'). I'm crazy about this miniature cutie. It flowers white blooms in the late winter, it doesn't want to grow out of its four-inch pot, yet its cinnamon-purple over cucumber-green leaves remain full atop fuzzy stalks. It's just so darn cute you want to pet it. A great plant for table tableaus because it fits into pottery and other nontraditional vessels.

CHAPTER FIFTEEN

BASIC GARDEN *thinking*

I am slightly embarrassed for the perfectionist gardener who claims that he or she is inspired by nature or strives for a measure of naturalism. Let's just be real for a minute. Gardeners despise nature in its natural state. The traditional New England garden has nothing to do with the indigenous landscape of a black-fly-and-mosquito-swarming pine forest; Palm Springs is as green as the midwestern plains thanks to the lawns and parks that obsure its true desert floor. Gardeners cannot even allow nature to run its course within the confines of their unnaturally contrived pieces of earth. We are constantly picking at our plantings, in order that they misbehave.

But that's what we're supposed to do; that's what gardens are, the premeditated, consistent reworking of the natural state. If that shocks you a little, don't think too much of it. It's human, which means it can be divine.

In this age of weekend garden makeovers, we've disregarded the larger importance and meaning of gardening, which, oddly enough, returns to tending nature. You cannot have a garden in forty-eight hours; all that gets you is a bit of outdoor set decorating. Gardening is so much more than that; it is a complex relationship that you build with your piece of earth over time. Time.

Indeed, the style of the garden is in how sweetly it keeps you in anxious anticipation.

I don't want to confuse you with too many pretty pictures in this chapter about gardening. Gardening is basically just three things, which have little to do with flowers, leaves, or even sunshine. I offer a back-to-basics primer that is the foundation of all great gardens, including yours.

the three big elements
WHAT GARDENING IS REALLY ABOUT

1. SOIL

Unlike untended land, the soil in a garden is cultivated and made as weed free as possible.

2. GEOMETRY

Lines define the areas of a garden. They all follow the gardener's linear formula.

3. INTERRUPTION

Gardens are meant to separate themselves from the larger natural landscape; otherwise, there would be no difference between backyards and woods.

the dirt on soil

THINK DIRT, NOT MULCH

If you've ever visited a garden anywhere in the world that most people would agree is grand, you may have noticed the dirt. It was spotless. The soil was so taken care of — revered — that it alone communicated a commitment to gardening as strong as that of the spectacular flower show. In America we love mulch. If you've paid close attention, the cable babble goes something like "Mulch with compost," but the visual is usually wood chips. They aren't the same; the former is for nutrition, the latter is for fudging — a weed barrier, a cover-up for bad cultivating.

It's okay to have mulch, but it should only be icing on the cake. The soil beneath it should be beautiful enough not to need it. You should also feed your soil with organic matter. If you don't have the time, space, or inclination to make your own compost, buy a commercially produced food, taking care that it is as free of chemicals as possible.

Though I am by far a nonminimalist, I admire gardens the most when they are stark and without flowers. It is in this state that they reveal your true style, which in a gardening sense means that your lawn, borders, and trees are given as much attention as you would give a glorious abundance of blooms.

Your soil is the foundation of your garden. Whenever you think you don't have enough flowers or your borders are too meager, get on your hands and knees to weed and cultivate your soil. The soil-gardener relationship is essential; without it, you don't really have a garden. Color and texture will be meaningless.

NO-MULCH BED

1. On a flat stretch of lawn, cut or dig out desired border.

2. Clean topsoil of roots, weeds, rocks, and debris.

3. Remove 2 to 3 inches of topsoil and reserve. The surface of new border should be 2 to 3 inches below turf line.

4. Dig out another 2 to 3 inches of dirt, and replace with previously removed topsoil.

5. Edge turf to create clean division.

2–3"

elementary geometry
HARD LINES

PERENNIAL EDGE

Hostas, in particular, make great edging for borders that abut lawns ranging from grass to asphalt. They suit the hardscape-focused gardener on a budget. Individual plants interlace nicely to create a low, soft hedge that sweeps the lawn, eliminating the need for hard edging such as brick or stone. In addition, hostas divide easily and are a steady and perennial source for new edging material.

EVERGREEN BORDER

A low hedge of evergreen by itself can be a satisfying border planting. The perception is that clipping is tedious, but when you weigh it against ever changing a perennial border that requires deadheading, dividing, augmentation with annuals, and winter preparation, a clipping every few months seems like cake.

SOFT LINES

THINK CANOPY, NOT HARDWARE

We often think too much about the accessory and not enough about the plant material. For climbing plants, I use rope and eye hooks as an invisible trellis.

INVISIBLE TRELLIS

1. Buy natural rope and eye hooks from the hardware store.

2. Install hooks at even intervals along wall or post, then string rope through loops. Plant your favorite climbing plant.

For more vigorous vines (roses, autumn clematis, etc.) use stronger rope and larger-gauge eye hooks.

THINK BARK, NOT LEAVES

A single tree can be all the garden you need. I'm speaking here about the simple yet sculptural possibilities of pruning. I always get a slight sense of foreboding every time someone starts a garden by cutting down a tree — for all the environmental reasons, of course, but also because it represents a lost opportunity.

Sometimes a well-pruned tree can be plenty of garden.

I am fortunate that I live adjacent to a park where this tree reminds me of how breathtaking one simple act can become.

interruption: containers

Buy annuals cheaply and early, and use them in different situations throughout the season.

CLASSICALLY STYLED CONTAINERS

The problem with borders is that we expect them to be ever-blooming shows. In the case of perennial borders, we load them with everything from crocus to dahlias, hoping for a steady stream of color. But none of these plants remains standing, and their fading is cruel and quick in comparison to the long wait between springs. With evergreen borders, we just go blah. It takes a mother's love to appreciate the exuberance of solid green plants.

Enter the container, a visual imposition that solidifies your mark on your garden. When placed in a border in the form of an urn, or any kind of classically inspired vessel elevated on a recognizable pedestal, it makes an engaging stage for your whims. A simple geranium plant in a border urn becomes spectacular, and while empty in the winter, it imparts a non-dormant, dynamic involvement.

Think of your annuals and perennials as mobile plants. Move them early or late in the season in a variety of ways.

ANNUALS

A cool thing about classically styled urns is that a lot of the houseplants in the flower section of your grocery store seem tailor-made for them; in fact, most plant material inside and outside provides plenty of material for your urns to be interesting year-round.

My personal rule for annuals is to buy as few of them as possible. Furthermore, they never stay in the same place throughout the growing season. If they start in the ground, I'll move them into different spots as the growing season progresses. Inevitably they end up as a centerpiece.

Though my garden is not organic in the strictest sense of the word, I do recycle.

Buy annuals cheaply and early, and use them in different situations throughout the season.

Think of your annuals and perennials as mobile plants. Move them early or late in the season in a variety of ways.

SPRING

I wait until the pansies get leggy and cheap at the garden center, then I combine them with coral bells that grow near the warm foundation. The coral bells just begin to bud when it's time to change to the early-summer plantings, and I cut back the pansies and put them in a pot, where they rest until they make noise again in the fall.

SUMMER

Tropical houseplants, croton, and bougainvillea come out and play on the street with marigolds.

FALL

I dig up hosta and sedum, pairing them with good old-fashioned dusty miller, which I keep around for the Thanksgiving table.

WINTER

I used to go crazy with squash and berries for our late autumn/winter look, but the kids in my neighborhood love to smash pumpkins as part of their extracurricular activities. One year I rescued this mugo pine from a too-wet situation, and it's wintered in the urn since, spending summers in a pot on the driveway.

found urnage and the high-low

The High-Low works in the border, too, and as long as you have a pot and a means to elevate it within the border, you're in business.

I found this driftwood table base on the curb on garbage day. The birdbath basin hung around for a while; neighborhood thieves stole the base a couple of years ago.

This hollowed old log was sitting on a nearby riverbank. I picked it up, buried one end into the border, and used the hollow end for a geranium.

This old chair sat in my basement waiting to be refinished. One day when I wanted to raise a terra-cotta pot in the border, I used it. And there it remains.

the tool rack
THE EIGHT ESSENTIALS

In order for the garden to yield exercise and meditative benefits, you need to simplify your tool collection according to the most basic functions. Other than a lawn mower, these are all you really need.

LEAF BROOM
Rids grass lawns of dead sod, handles fall leaf drops and spring cleanup.

RAKE
An efficient cultivator can work around seedlings and comb through rocky soil.

HEDGE TRIMMER
Use for evening out evergreens. An excellent tool for trimming grass near borders.

SHOVEL
Find a reliable steel shovel.

LOPPER
Use for larger twigs and shrub shaping.

SAW
Use for larger branches and serious pruning.

HAND-HELD TRIMMER
Use for flowers, small twigs, and branches, both indoors and out.

EDGING SPADE
Keeps borders clean and free.

OPPOSITE: You don't need pea gravel or stone paths to create a stunning garden room. Bring out your best chairs, and place them on the asphalt near your border. Place tables within the border for a truly charming tablescape, instead of faking it with unnecessary accessories that amount to crap.

CHAPTER SIXTEEN

KEEPING THINGS *pretty*

When I was in the restaurant business, people used to be intimidated to invite us over for lunch or dinner. They'd worry about what to cook, how to set the table — so everything was "just so." Inevitably they'd venture into new cooking territory (which always spelled disaster), but even if the results were delicious, they'd be so filled with anxiety about their tablescapes that we'd be uncomfortable, too. By contrast, one of our waitresses lived down the street in a tiny, messy house. One day she invited us over for tacos in the crispy El Paso shells, which she served on her only plates, some really exquisite old china. Needless to say, she became one of our most treasured friends.

Life happens quickly. **You should use your best things every day no matter where you live and what that "best" happens to be.** If you have "everyday" dishes, "good" dishes, and yet more sets that are food-specific, you have too much. Pick the best set (especially something you've had in your family), and give the others away. Live like the king or queen in your own kingdom.

If you ask me, the reason we don't appreciate all the things we have is that we put most of them away for the big "what if" and for special occasions. Home-show hosts talk more about entertaining than actual living. Well, you and I don't entertain every day or even every week. We shouldn't live as though the best we have to offer weren't good enough for ourselves and our families.

Live well by using your best things. Become intimate with every inch of your home and all things in it by getting down and dirty with them. By that I mean not only should you use them well, but you should also clean them with the same gusto. You must, really.

cleaning by the equinox

Twice a year, in the spring (around March 21) and the fall (September 22), your home should be cleaned from top to bottom. It is physiologically natural and psychologically necessary. In this day of disposable mops, hands-free vacuum cleaners, liquid fresh air, and affordable housekeeping services — all of which are instant — it is too easy to forget that we need to care for things personally in order to have an authentic relationship with them. This is what gives you style. More important, you become less prone to the nonsense makeover when you really appreciate your things.

If this seems overwhelming — and to some it is — you only need to remember three things. The best cleaning is broken down into three basic actions: dusting, washing, and restoring.

THE ONE-ROOM RULE

Do not undertake more than one room, or else you'll fudge. Although you will use two adjacent rooms at the same time, emptying as much of the room being cleaned as you can, don't feel compelled to clean both.

THE DON'T-MIX-STEPS RULE

Don't confuse dusting with washing. Dusting is a dry process; washing is a wet one. Dusting your ceiling fan is different from washing your ceiling fan.

OPPOSITE: It's not enough to say you appreciate your things. Pick up every object you own and wipe it down.

DUSTING FROM TOP TO BOTTOM

Supplies:

- CLEAN, DRY PAINTBRUSH
- DRY CLOTHS
- LADDER
- CLEAN BROOM
- VACUUM CLEANER
- DUST MASK AND PROTECTIVE GOGGLES, IF NECESSARY

STEP 1. EMPTY THE ROOM

Remove all items from walls and shelves, roll up rugs and take them out, remove washable curtains. If you can, try to completely empty the room; but if that's impossible, push whatever you can to the center of the room, and cover it with an old blanket or drop cloth.

STEP 2. DUST CEILING, WALLS, AND WINDOWSILLS

Use a washed, clean broom to sweep the ceiling while standing on the floor. Use a dry paintbrush along the corners where the ceiling and walls meet. Wipe the ceiling fan's blades with a soft, dry cloth, and brush the motor and light fixtures with the paintbrush. If you can, vacuum as much of the walls as your attachments will allow. Also vacuum windowsills, blinds/shades, and drapes.

STEP 3. DUST BASEBOARDS AND FLOORS

Use the paintbrush to dust the baseboard, especially where it meets the walls and the floor or in any decorative crevice. Dust radiators well, vacuuming out dust bunnies. Vacuum

A clean, dry paintbrush is a fantastic dusting tool.

and sweep the entire floor, and remove dust that has settled on the drop cloth that covers the things you couldn't move out of the room.

WASHING ROOMS FROM TOP TO BOTTOM

Supplies:

- CLEAN CLOTHS
- BUCKET
- WARM WATER
- SPIC AND SPAN OR OTHER CLEANER
- RUBBER GLOVES
- ELECTRIC FAN TO CIRCULATE AIR FOR QUICKER DRYING
- CLEAN TOWEL FOR KNEE COMFORT
- MOP WITH CLEAN HEAD

STEP 1. WASH WALLS, WINDOWSILLS, AND TRIM

Starting at the top of your walls, wipe with cloths dipped in a bucket of cleaning water, using even pressure. Be sure to rinse and wring regularly, changing the water when it gets brown.

STEP 2. WASH BASEBOARDS BY HAND

Resist the temptation to mop your baseboards. Get on your knees, and wash them with fresh cleaning water, washing the floor itself about 2 to 4 inches in (these edges of the floor tend to build up dirt that regular mopping misses).

Forget mops twice a year and get on your hands and knees to scrub your floors.

STEP 3. WASH FLOORS

If you can do it, I recommend washing the floors by hand, kneeling on a towel for comfort. It's a great ab and arm workout. Otherwise, mop with a new, clean mop head. Note: If you have things in the middle of the room, move them to wash the floor, but return them to the center when the floor is dry.

WASHING WINDOWS

Supplies:

- SQUEEGEE
- BUCKET
- WARM WATER
- WHITE VINEGAR
- PAPER TOWELS
- NEWSPAPER
- CLEAN RAZOR BLADES

WASHING RECIPE

4 gallons warm water

½ cup white vinegar

¼ cup dishwashing liquid

STEP 1. FIRST WASH

Generously wash the interior glass the with washing recipe and cloth, razoring off any hard spots. Squeegee clean.

STEP 2. SECOND WASH

Wash again with clean water. Squeegee, and then, using gently crushed newspaper, wipe the glass in a circular motion. Wipe the edges of the windows and windowsills with clean paper towels or rags.

STEP 3. GET RID OF THE SOUR VINEGAR SMELL

If you don't mind the smell, no problem; it dissipates with a bit of air circulation. But if you don't like the smell of vinegar, light a match or two.

STEP 4. EXTERIOR OF WINDOWS

If you can wash the exterior glass safely from the inside (i.e., your windows flip inside for safe washing), then do so. However, if you need to go outside, be sure to use caution if you need a ladder.

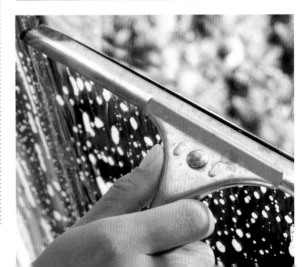

STEP 5. SCREENS AND STORMS

If cleaning in the fall, wash screens and put them away. Wash storm windows before installing them for the season.

If cleaning in the spring, replace removable storm windows with freshly washed and dry screens. If storms are part of the window system, be sure that they are washed on both sides.

Foam cleaners and conditioners are great for leather furniture.

RESTORING FROM TOP TO BOTTOM

Supplies:

- PAINT AND BRUSHES
- GLUE
- LADDER
- MOP
- BUCKET AND CLEANER
- WOOD POLISH

Keep wallpaper looking good with regular attention.

STEP 1. PAINT TOUCH-UP

If there are any spots you'd like to touch up, do so using a brush, not a roller. Feather out lightly with a mostly dry brush so that it looks seamless when dry. Touch up painted baseboards and windowsills if desired.

STEP 2. PAPER TOUCH-UP

If wallpaper seems to have loosened, use glue to reseal, rubbing with a damp cloth to even out.

STEP 3. TREAT WOOD

If you have natural wood finishes on your baseboards or window trim, use your preference of wood wax or oil/sealer to give a light treatment.

STEP 4. FINISH FLOOR

Wax or treat the floor as you traditionally do.

TWO NATURAL WAYS TO CLEAN RUGS AND CARPETS

While there are many professional ways to clean area rugs, I find that a good vacuum and some help from Mother Nature are good for poly, wool, cotton, and sisal or jute rugs.

SUMMER SUNBATH

1. Vacuum the rug.
2. Remove stains as recommended by the manufacturer.
3. Wash the rug by vigorously rubbing it with a clean cloth dampened only by water (or machine wash cotton rugs as directed).
4. Completely dry the rug topside down in the sun by laying it on a clean patch of grass or over a line. When mostly dry, turn it faceup to the sun for a maximum of one hour (to prevent bleaching).
5. When the rug is returned to the room, lightly mist it with perfumed water (such as lavender or rose water) or a watered dilution (20 parts water to 1 part scent in a spray bottle) of your favorite scent.

WINTER SNOW SHOWER

This is especially excellent for animal-hide rugs (pony, shaggy wool, etc.) or for old, delicate rugs you want to keep out of the sun.

Repeat steps 1 and 2 above.

3. Take rug outside and throw onto fresh, dry snow. Vigorously brush snowflakes deep into both sides of rug with clean broom or stiff brush (be gentle with more delicate rugs). The snow will absorb the dirt in the carpet or rug fibers and fall away.
4. Beat carpet or rug well to remove all snow. Return to room and dab snowmelt, if any.

ALL THE THINGS YOU CAN CLEAN WITH A PAINTBRUSH

A clean paintbrush used exclusively for dusting is a cool, helpful tool that has a variety of uses. When followed with wiping by a water-dampened cloth and a final drying wipe with a clean dry cloth, it's amazing how many things come quite clean.

- **BOOKS**
- **LAMP SHADES**
- **PICTURE FRAMES**
- **DRAPERY**
- **REMOTE CONTROLS**
- **COMPUTERS**
- **STEREO EQUIPMENT**
- **LIGHT FIXTURES**
- **TELEVISIONS**
- **ANTIQUE WOOD FURNITURE**

basic cleaning supplies:
an uncluttered look

THE DUSTERS
All you need are a
vacuum cleaner, a
mop, clean rags,
paper towels, a
broom, a paintbrush,
and a soft duster.

THE CLEANERS

An ammonia-based all-purpose cleaner, an all-purpose stain remover, and scouring powder.

THE POLISHERS

Leather conditioner, wood conditioner, floor wax, metal polish, and glass cleaner.

THE EASY-TO-MISS LIST

STOVE, MICROWAVE, AND SMALL KITCHEN APPLIANCES These appliances should be deep-cleaned as often as once a month; however, a quick trick for stoves and microwaves is to spray glass cleaner right after use. It not only cleans but it also shines surfaces. Blenders, juicers, spice grinders, and so on should always be cleaned and dried after every use. And don't forget to turn your toaster upside down to shake out the crumbs.

REFRIGERATORS AND FREEZERS Refrigerators should *always* be clean. Crispers should be regularly emptied of wilted vegetables and fruit and removed and hand washed in the sink. Shelves should be wiped down often, as open containers tend to leave rings. Jars of food should also be regularly wiped and the lids rinsed. Food frozen for more than six months ought to be thrown out or eaten, and ice cubes should be used quickly or remade if not used within one month.

"AIR" APPLIANCES For air conditioners, fans, and washers and dryers, a quick, simple sweep for dust in their vents, sides, and backs is easily accomplished with a dry cloth and a vacuum cleaner. Again, a clean paintbrush comes in handy.

GARBAGE CANS AND HAMPERS These should be washed out and dried at least every four months. Garbage bags often leak, so cans may have to be washed out more often. To help keep hampers as clean as possible, do not put wet clothes directly into a hamper. Instead, dry them over a railing outside or a chair, and place them directly in the washer to launder.

HOUSEPLANTS A good shower in the tub keeps plants from accumulating dust. Be sure they are dry and drained well before putting them back in place.

BED PILLOWS Every three months or so, replace pillow liners and toss the pillows themselves into the dryer after wiping them with a damp cloth. In the summer, give them a good sunbathing as well.

BROOMS AND BRUSHES You have to clean these if you expect them to do their job right. Vacuum bristles and brushes, and hose them down (outside or in the shower), then dip in a pail of soapy water with a touch of bleach. Rinse well, shake, and allow to drip-dry.

VACUUM CLEANER It's not just about changing the bags. Brush the vacuum heads, freeing dust, hair, threads, and lint. Wash plastic attachments in the dishwasher. Wipe down the body and inside the canister with a cloth dipped in detergent water. Wipe clean before replacing the attachments.

UNDER THE SINK Empty all the undersink cabinets, and wash them down with soapy water. Wipe clean, and allow to air-dry, then replace the contents, which have themselves been wiped down.

TELEPHONES These are some of the most undercleaned appliances in the house. Wipe button pads, receivers, and cords with bleach-added spray to keep the cooties and dust in check.

BE HERE NOW

COMMUNITY GARDEN

Parks and Recreation Department

CHAPTER SEVENTEEN

CHARISMA: HOW THEY *feel*

The worst pairing of words in the history of language has got to be, hands down, *blissful ignorance*. It's a condition that we've adopted to mask the outrageousness of apathy, believing that it's actually fashionable. An expression whose meaning is tantamount to Marie Antoinette's "Let them eat cake" is an accurate depiction of what we do to ourselves — when we choose not to know, we stick our heads up our asses. I personally can't stand it. I don't accept it from my friends, and I won't accept it from myself.

Consider for a moment the cycle of blissful ignorance. Let's take your neighbors. For a complex of reasons, you choose not to know or be involved with the people living next door to you, and you go out of your way to avoid them. Already you've allowed a level of fear into your daily life. Then one day they do something you don't agree with — let's say they play loud music at a backyard cookout. That fear turns into anger. You decide to get even and throw an even louder party. Eventually you fight, and then it becomes nasty and practically irreconcilable. All because you chose not to know how your neighbor fit into your perfect life.

Ignorance becomes fear becomes anger becomes evil. That's just the way it is, I didn't make it up. This is an extreme example, of course, but when it comes to your house, garden, food, entertaining, and personal style, the equation plays out the exact same way. Take weddings. No matter how visually stunning the bride is on her wedding day, if she went about it being a complete and utter Bridezilla, she will remain so in the eyes of her loved ones who endured it.

In the previous chapter, I outlined how to achieve an outward style that people find irresistible. Now I will discuss the emotional and spiritual qualities — known as charisma — that round out iconic style.

the four dynamics of charisma

DYNAMIC NO. 1. UNDERSTAND THE MYTHICAL JOURNEY

You do not need to have a philosophy degree or even to be educated by western standards to understand that every person who ever lived and will live undertakes the same life journey. It doesn't matter if you're Chinese or Piedmontese, Muslim or Catholic, Republican or Democrat, rich or poor, fat or skinny, healthy or ill. We share birth, growth, and death, and during our lifetimes we will seek ways to explain how we feel and what we hope for.

Objects have a journey as well. Homes, whether they are tin shacks, caves, or Bel Air mansions, all function to shelter, comfort, and stabilize. Knives, pots and pans, sofas, beds, and washbasins are an intrinsic part of our journey. And they ought to be respected on this basis *first* and not merely viewed as things to make over and dispose of when some screaming decorating diva has to pay the rent.

mother's finest evening bag for your gala events; honoring your father's choice of how to dress and not pressuring him to get a makeover. This is *gai*.

When I was a kid, I poked innocent fun at a mentally retarded child, as many kids do. My elders responded with a swift, open-handed slap of my face that did two things. I realized that I was wrong, but in that moment I also felt the pain of exclusion, probably similar to the kid and those who loved him. I am grateful for the knowledge that moment gave me. I'm not saying you should slap your kid — of course not. But you must not allow any blissful ignorance to go unchecked.

DYNAMIC NO. 2. RECOGNIZE YOUR TRIBE

One of my very good friends, Phyllis, once said to me, "Dan, you and I belong to the same cosmic tribe." Now, in many ways, Phyllis and I couldn't be more different. First of all, she's

During our lifetimes we will seek ways to explain how we feel and what we hope for. Objects have a journey as well.

When you respect and understand the mythical journey, you are open to having true iconic style. A lovely cobblestone street in Europe with apartments whose only garden is a flower box in a window; wearing your

about twenty years older than I am. She loves the Beatles, and I'm constantly humiliated for being a Mariah Carey fan. Our politics are as disparate as night and day. I'm a Catholic, and she's devoutly religiously unorganized. Yet we meet, and we're good friends, and we love each other. At the same time, I know people who share political and religious beliefs with me who are not part of my tribe. You simply cannot rely on surface profiling to fashion your guest list.

If you can let go of hanging out with the "right" crowd for the "right" reasons, you not only harvest the breadth of the world's potential for friendship, but you are also in constant practice of tolerance. You become confounding to strangers, which makes you iconic.

DYNAMIC NO. 3. STEP OUTSIDE

When you understand the mythical journey and have the ability to recognize others beyond the surface, it's time to get out of your comfort zone and understand loneliness. I'm not saying to chuck your entire life and abandon your loved ones to spend four years in the desert; I'm saying think about it. You can simply put on a record and immerse yourself in the messages of the songs. Or read poetry not for the rhyme, but for the poem's reason. This awareness changes you in a way that no makeover can.

DYNAMIC NO. 4. COME HOME

In other words, forgive. Your folks may not ever understand your lifestyle or style statement, but it's okay. It was all well and good to rebel against your mother's store-bought ice-cream cake in favor of tiramisu. It is appropriate to insist on washable slipcovers rather than emulating the irrational reverence of your grandmother's off-limits living room. But style does not exist in a vacuum; at some point you must reconcile with your history. Remember, legacy and emotion are almost 50 percent of style.

For me, it's Spam and rice. For as much caviar and cashmere that I've been lucky enough to experience, frying up some Spam and eating it with a plate of plain white rice keeps me grounded. The U.S. soldiers brought it to Guam after the Japanese occupations, and it trickled down the generations as a favorite, if culinarily unpopular, staple. I don't care — I wouldn't be alive if it weren't around. So I eat it as a ritual remembrance first and as a subversive style statement second.

emulation versus inspiration: how to remain original

Herein lies the conundrum that all of us must face, whether we are slaves to design or stylin' in the truest, *gai*est ways. For in the realm of house, garden, food, entertaining, and personal style, nothing is really original. There hasn't been an original thought in years, perhaps centuries. I like to think I'm original, but curly hair's been around a long time, as have cat's-eye frames.

It's all been done. Don't we all know that boiling pasta for seven minutes per pound gives you al dente? That when you plant bulbs in the fall, you get flowers in the spring? That a higher thread count on your skin feels much better than sheets with a less dense weave?

The honest truth is that your spirit is the most original thing about you, and so you must constantly nourish it with family, friends, and love. But the spirit needs both a body and a mind to make a style statement; attend to your image, and hone your charisma.

You see, one of the subconscious mechanisms of *gai* is this very idea of a triple threat, this trinity — spirit, body, and intellect. It is a paradigm used by early Christian religions to explain divinity; yet it is also something that we're searching for when we so easily call someone a domestic goddess. *Goddess* should actually have more meaning than being a crazy, glue-gun-toting, baking-mad woman. Intelligent style requires body and spirit. This merger has eluded us for much too long.

Your spirit is your style. That's all it ever was or will be.

hone your charisma: six vital activities

1. STALK A FINE ART

Find a form of dance, theater, music, or representational art that appeals to you, and focus on it exclusively as a fun pastime.

Hip-hop, Latin (flamenco, salsa, mariachi, etc.), Chinese, ballet, modern, tap, jazz, Broadway, Chekhov, El Greco, Rockwell Kent, Ben Shahn, Edward Curtis, early American quilts, and Native American pottery.

2. VOLUNTEER

And I'm not just talking about a one-time walkathon to raise money that replaces your workout. I'm talking about something out of your comfort zone.

Community garden, children's hospital, old-folks home, ASPCA, local fire station, soup kitchen, homeless shelter, library, school, immigration organizations, school committees, multiple sclerosis, veterans' homes, historical societies.

OPPOSITE: I'm over crème brûlée. But a Beethoven sonata for dessert? Now that's style.

3. REDISCOVER THE HUMANITIES

Take an adult-ed course at your local community college on religion, philosophy, language, literature, or culture.

 Jung, Freud, Saint Augustine, Italian, Edna St. Vincent Millay, Homer's *Odyssey,* Chaucer, Shakespeare, the Zuni tribe, the Abenaki of New England, Southern Baptists, poetry writing class, sonnets, haiku, simile/metaphor.

4. BE INVOLVED IN COMMUNITY

Do you know who your local government is? Where do they live, and how did they get into office? Get to know the inner workings of your neighborhood.

 Alderman, selectman, tax cap, tax rate, school board, water committee, commercial zone, residential zone, streets and sanitation, community policing, utilities, easement, registrar, township, charter, tax credits.

5. DO WITHOUT

Every time you think you need something nonessential, ask yourself, "Do I really need this?" Then try to do without.

 Eat at home, water instead of wine, fruit instead of cake, last season's bag, visit the cobbler, save money, library instead of video store, phone call instead of notecards, a long walk instead of a massage, a book instead of a movie.

6. ADOPT AN OUTCAST

It might be a pet, but it ought to be a person. If you know of a foreign student or an elderly person living alone, make him or her part of your life.

 Mentally disabled, Big Brother or Big Sister, widowed aunt, three-legged dog, a sidewalk that needs weeding, graffiti that needs cleaning, a merchant who could use a customer-service clue.

. . . ask yourself, "Do I really need this?" Then try to do without.

EPILOGUE

At the beginning of this book, I issued a style check — do you remember it? Name three things that represent your style. The first one had to be free; it had to have cost you nothing. The second one had to have cost you under one hundred dollars; and the third had to have been at the top range of your budget when you got it. Have your answers changed from the beginning of the book? Mine are on the following page.

the 3-things test: my answers

1.

FREEBIE

My hair. As a kid I hated it, and as an adult I tried all the methods to rebuke it, from shaving my head to corn rows to chemical straightening. Over the last five years or so, I just decided to let it do its thing. As a style statement, it's pretty hard to ignore its singularity.

2.

UNDER $100

My plain gold wedding band that I bought at deep discount. I wore it on my left hand for nearly fourteen years, and now it's around my neck. Its added significance is as a remembrance of my dad, who passed away as I was planning this book. It represents family, the homes of my life. It's also a reminder of my life's work: when all is said and done, I want to be remembered as the guy who drew the line between perfection and living in meaningful, true style.

3.

TOP-END

My glasses. Until I found them a few years ago, I'd never spent so much money on a pair, nor was I ever so loyal to a single style. They're cat's eye–shaped, so they're a bit last century, traditional but humorous. They're handmade in France, and I like that quiet, unostentatious luxury. People don't need to tour my home or look in my closet to figure out that I am a champion of individual style — my glasses say it for me.

Ready? Get set. Gai.
Your irresistible true style awaits you.

ACKNOWLEDGMENTS

My sincerest gratitude to Maureen Egen, for her initial interest in my work and for introducing it to my publisher, Jill Cohen, who quickly became an advocate and renegade believer.

To my editor, Kristen Schilo, for her recognition, guidance, and friendship.

To designer Kay Shuckhart, for her willing collaboration; to John Labbé for his conceptual inspiration and unique vision; and to Leela Corman for her groovy illustration on page 130.

To my photographer, François Gagne, whose camaraderie, hard work, and dedication helped create the visual element of my message; to Monica Wendel, for her technical generosity and goonie pledge; to Jessica Lockhart and Darrell Bradbury for everything.

To Lisa Dubrow and Mat Tombers, my HOmies.

To Jenny Drilon, my beautiful former wife, for her inspiration and support.

INDEX

Dan Ho is the publisher and creator of *Rescue Magazine* and has been called "the anti-Martha" by *Time* magazine and *USA Today*. In 2006 Ho will host a series on Discovery Health network, as well as four one-hour specials.